EGYPTIAN LANGUAGE

Easy Lessons in Egyptian Hieroglyphics

with Sign List

SIR E. A. WALLIS BUDGE

Dorset Press
New York

To

HENRY EDWARD JULER, ESQUIRE, F.R.C.S.

ETC., ETC., ETC.

TO WHOSE SKILL AND KINDNESS

MY EYESIGHT OWES SO MUCH

This edition published by Dorset Press,
a division of Barnes & Noble, Inc.

1993 Dorset Press

ISBN 1-56619-060-6

Printed and bound in the United States of America

M 9 8 7 6 5 4 3 2 1

PREFACE.

———◦◦◦———

THIS little book is intended to form an easy intro-
duction to the study of the Egyptian hieroglyphic inscriptions, and has been prepared in answer to many
requests made both in Egypt and in England. It con-
tains a short account of the decipherment of Egyptian
hieroglyphics, and a sketch of the hieroglyphic system
of writing and of the general principles which underlie
the use of picture signs to express thought. The main
facts of Egyptian grammar are given in a series of
short chapters, and these are illustrated by numerous
brief extracts from hieroglyphic texts ; each extract is
printed in hieroglyphic type and is accompanied by
a transliteration and translation. Following the example of the early Egyptologists it has been thought
better to multiply extracts from texts rather than to
heap up a large number of grammatical details without
supplying the beginner with the means of examining
their application. In the limits of the following pages

it would be impossible to treat Egyptian grammar at any length, while the discussion of details would be quite out of place. The chief object has been to make the beginner familiar with the most common signs and words, so that he may, whilst puzzling out the extracts from texts quoted in illustration of grammatical facts, be able to attack the longer connected texts given in my "First Steps in Egyptian" and in my "Egyptian Reading Book".

Included in this book is a lengthy list of hieroglyphic characters with their values both as phonetics and ideograms. Some of the characters have not yet been satisfactorily identified and the correctness of the positions of these is, in consequence, doubtful; but it has been thought best to follow both the classification, even when wrong, and the numbering of the characters which are found in the list of "Hieroglyphen" printed by Herr Adolf Holzhausen of Vienna.

E. A. WALLIS BUDGE.

CONTENTS.

———

CHAPTER I.

HIEROGLYPHIC WRITING.

THE ancient Egyptians expressed their ideas in writing by means of a large number of picture signs which are commonly called Hieroglyphics. They began to use them for this purpose more than seven thousand years ago, and they were employed uninterruptedly until about B. C. 100, that is to say, until nearly the end of the rule of the Ptolemies over Egypt. It is hardly probable that the hieroglyphic system of writing was invented in Egypt, and the evidence on this point now accumulating indicates that it was brought there by certain invaders who came from north-east or central Asia; they settled down in the valley of the Nile at some place between Memphis on the north and Thebes on the south, and gradually established their civilization and religion in their new home. Little by little the writing spread to the north and to the south, until at length hieroglyphics were employed, for state purposes at least, from the coast

of the Mediterranean to the most southern portion of
the Island of Meroë, that is to say, over a tract of
country more than 2000 miles long. A remarkable
peculiarity of Egyptian hieroglyphics is the slight mo-
dification of form which they suffered during a period
of thousands of years, a fact due, no doubt, partly to
the material upon which the Egyptians inscribed them,
and partly to a conservatism begotten of religious con-
victions. The Babylonian and Chinese picture characters became modified at so early a period that, some
thousands of years before Christ, their original forms
were lost. This reference to the modified forms of
hieroglyphics brings us at once to the mention of the
various ways in which they were written in Egypt,
i. e., to the three different kinds of Egyptian writing.

The oldest form of writing is the **hieroglyphic,** in
which the various objects, animate and inanimate, for
which the characters stand are depicted as accurately
as possible. The following titles of one Ptaḥ-ḥetep,
who lived at the period of the rule of the IVth dynasty
will explain this; by the side of each hieroglyphic is
its description.

1.[1] ⬭ a mouth
2. ▣ a door made of planks of wood fastened
together by three cross-pieces
3. ⌐ᴅ the fore-arm and hand

---

[1] The brackets shew the letters which, when taken together,
form words.

4. a lion's head and one fore paw stretched out

5. see No. 3

6. doorway surmounted by cornice of small serpents

7. a jackal

8. a kind of water fowl

9. an owl

10. a growing plant

11. a cake

12. a reed to which is tied a scribe's writing tablet or palette, having two hollows in it for red and black ink

13. see No. 9

14. see No. 1

15. the breast of a man with the two arms stretched out

16. see No. 11

17. a seated man holding a basket upon his head.

In the above examples of picture signs the objects which they represent are tolerably evident, but a large number of hieroglyphics do not so easily lend themselves to identification. Hieroglyphics were cut in stone, wood, and other materials with marvellous accuracy, at depths varying from $^1/_{16}$ of an inch to 1 inch; the details of the objects represented were given either by cutting or by painting in colours. In the earliest times the mason must have found it easier to cut characters into the stone than to sculpture them in relief; but it is probable that the idea of preserving carefully what had been inscribed also entered his mind, for frequently when the surface outline of a character has been destroyed sufficient traces remain in the incuse portion of it for purposes of identification. Speaking generally, celestial objects are coloured blue, as also are metal vessels and instruments; animals, birds, and reptiles are painted as far as possible to represent their natural colours; the Egyptian man is painted red, and the woman yellow or a pinky-brown colour; and so on. But though in some cases the artist endeavoured to make each picture sign an exact representation of the original object in respect of shape or form and colour, with the result that the simplest inscription became a splendid piece of ornamentation in which the most vivid colours blended harmoniously, in the majority of painted texts which have been preserved to us the artists have not been consistent in the colouring of their signs. Frequently the same tints of a colour are not used for the same picture, an entirely different colour being often employed; and it is hard not to think that the artist or scribe, having come to the end of the paint which should have been employed for one class of hieroglyphics, frequently made use of that which should have been reserved for another. It has been said that many of the objects which are represented by picture signs may be identified by means of the colours with which they are painted, and this is, no doubt, partly true; but the inconsistency of the Egyptian artist often does away entirely with the value of the colour as a means of identification.

Picture signs or hieroglyphics were employed for religious and state purposes from the earliest to the latest times, and it is astonishing to contemplate the labour which must have been expended by the mason in cutting an inscription of any great length, if every character was well and truly made. Side by side with cutters in stone carvers in wood must have existed, and for a proof of the skill which the latter class of handicraftsmen possessed at a time which must be well nigh pre-dynastic, the reader is referred to the beautiful panels in the Gizeh Museum which have been published by Mariette.[1] The hieroglyphics and figures of the deceased are in relief, and are most delicately and beautifully executed;

[1] See *Les Mastaba de l'Ancien Empire.* Paris, 1882, v. 74 ff.

but the unusual grouping of the characters proves that
they belong to a period when as yet dividing lines for
facilitating the reading of the texts had not been in-
troduced. These panels cannot belong to a period
later than the IIIrd, and they are probably earlier than
the Ist dynasty. Inscriptions in stone and wood were
cut with copper or bronze and iron chisels. But the
Egyptians must have had need to employ their hieroglyphics for other purposes than inscriptions which
were intended to remain in one place, and the official
documents of state, not to mention the correspondence
of the people, cannot have been written upon stone or
wood. At a very early date the papyrus plant[1] was
made into a sort of paper upon which were written
drafts of texts which the mason had to cut in stone,
official documents, letters, etc. The stalk of this plant,
which grew to the height of twelve or fifteen feet, was
triangular, and was about six inches in diameter in its
thickest part. The outer rind was removed from it,
and the stalk was divided into layers with a flat needle;
these layers were laid upon a board, side by side, and
upon these another series of layers was laid in a
horizontal direction, and a thin solution of gum was
then run between them, after which both series of
layers were pressed and dried. The number of such
sheets joined together depended upon the length of the
roll required. The papyrus rolls which have come

---

[1] *Byblus hieraticus*, or *Cyperus papyrus*.

down to us vary greatly in length and width; the finest
Theban papyri are about seventeen inches wide, and
the longest roll yet discovered is the great Papyrus
of Rameses III,[1] which measures one hundred and
thirty-five feet in length. On such rolls of papyrus the
Egyptians wrote with a reed, about ten inches long
and one eighth of an inch in diameter, the end of
which was bruised to make the fibres flexible, and
not cut; the ink was made of vegetable substances, or
of coloured earths mixed with gum and water.

Now it is evident that the hieroglyphics traced in
outline upon papyrus with a comparatively blunt reed
can never have had the clearness and sharp outlines
of those cut with metal chisels in a hard substance;
it is also evident that the increased speed at which
government orders and letters would have to be written
would cause the scribe, unconsciously at first, to ab-
breviate and modify the picture signs, until at length
only the most salient characteristics of each remained.
And this is exactly what happened. Little by little the
hieroglyphics lost much of their pictorial character, and
degenerated into a series of signs which went to form
the cursive writing called Hieratic. It was used ex-
tensively by the priests in copying literary works in
all periods, and though it occupied originally a subordinate position in respect of hieroglyphics, especially
as regards religious texts, it at length became equal in

---

[1] Harris Papyrus, No. 1. British Museum, No. 9999.

importance to hieroglyphic writing. The following example of hieratic writing is taken from the Prisse Papyrus upon which at a period about B. C. 2600 two texts, containing moral precepts which were composed about one thousand years earlier, were written.

Now if we transcribe these into hieroglyphics we obtain the following :—

1.   a reed
2.   a mouth
3.   a hare
4.   the wavy surface of water
5.   see No. 4
6.   a kind of vessel
7.   an owl
8.   a bolt of a door
9.   a seated figure of a man
10.   a stroke written to make the word symmetrical

11.   see No. 1
12.   a knee bone (?)
13.   see No. 2.
14.   a roll of papyrus tied up
15.   an eye
16.   see No. 6
17.   a goose
18.   see No. 9
19.   see No. 4
20.   a chair back
21.   a sickle

22. an eagle

23. see No. 7

24. a tree

25. see No. 14

26. an axe

27. see No. 10.

On comparing the above hieroglyphics with their hieratic equivalents it will be seen that only long practice would enable the reader to identify quickly the abbreviated characters which he had before him; the above specimen of hieratic is, however, well written and is relatively easy to read. In the later times, *i. e.,* about B. C. 900, the scribes invented a series of purely arbitrary or conventional modifications of the hieratic characters and so a new style of writing, called Enchorial or Demotic, came into use; it was used chiefly for business or social purposes at first, but at length copies of the "Book of the Dead" and lengthy literary compositions were written in it. In the Ptolemaic period Demotic was considered to be of such importance that whenever the text of a royal decree was inscribed upon a stele which was to be set up in some public place and was intended to be read by the public in general, a version of the said decree, written in the Demotic character, was added. Famous examples of stelae inscribed in hieroglyphic, demotic, and Greek, are the Canopus Stone, set up at Canopus in the reign of Ptolemy III. Euergetes I. in the ninth year of his reign (B. C. 247—222), and the Rosetta

Stone set up at Rosetta, in the eighth year of the reign of Ptolemy V. Epiphanes (B. C. 205—182).

In all works on ancient Egyptian grammar the reader will find frequent reference to *Coptic*. The Coptic language is a dialect of Egyptian of which four or five varieties are known; its name is derived from the name of the old Egyptian city Qebt, through the Arabic *Qubṭ*, which in its turn was intended to represent the Gr. Αἴγυπτος. The dialect dates from the second century of our era, and the literature written in it is chiefly Christian. Curiously enough Coptic is written with the letters of the Greek alphabet, to which were added six characters, derived from the Demotic forms of ancient Egyptian hieroglyphics, to express sounds which were peculiar to the Egyptian language.

Hieroglyphic characters may be written in columns or in horizontal lines, which are sometimes to be read from left to right and sometimes from right to left. There was no fixed rule about the direction in which the characters should be written, and as we find that in inscriptions which are cut on the sides of a door they usually face inwards, *i. e.,* towards the door, each group thus facing the other, the scribe and sculptor needed only to follow their own ideas in the arrangement and direction of the characters, or the dictates of symmetry. To ascertain the direction in which an inscription is to be read we must observe in which way the men, and birds, and animals face, and then read *towards* them. The two following examples will illustrate this :—

Now on looking at these passages we notice that the men, the chicken, the owls, the hawk, and the hares all face to the left; to read these we must read from left to right, *i. e., towards* them. The second extract has been set up by the compositor with the characters

facing in the opposite direction, so that to read these
now we must read from right to left (No. 3).

Hieratic is usually written in horizontal lines which
are to be read from right to left, but in some papyri
dating from the XIIth dynasty the texts are arranged
in short columns.

Before we pass to the consideration of the Egyptian
Alphabet, syllabic signs, etc., it will be necessary to
set forth briefly the means by which the power to read
these was recovered, and to sketch the history of the
decipherment of Egyptian hieroglyphics in connection
with the Rosetta Stone.

CHAPTER II

The Rosetta Stone was found by a French artillery officer called Boussard, among the ruins of Fort Saint Julien, near the Rosetta mouth of the Nile, in 1799, but it subsequently came into the possession of the British Government at the capitulation of Alexandria. It now stands at the southern end of the great Egyptian Gallery in the British Museum. The top and right hand bottom corner of this remarkable object have been broken off, and at the present the texts inscribed upon it consist of fourteen lines of hieroglyphics, thirty-two lines of demotic, and fifty-four lines of Greek. It measures about 3 ft. 9 in. $\times$ 2 ft. $4^1/_2$ in. $\times$ 11 in. on the inscribed side.

The Rosetta Stone records that Ptolemy V. Epiphanes, king of Egypt from B. C. 205 to B. C. 182, conferred great benefits upon the priesthood, and set aside large revenues for the maintenance of the temples, and remitted the taxes due from the people at a period of

distress, and undertook and carried out certain costly
engineering works in connection with the irrigation
system of Egypt. In gratitude for these acts the priesthood convened a meeting at Memphis, and ordered
that a statue of the king should be set up in every
temple of Egypt, that a gilded wooden statue of the
king placed in a gilded wooden shrine should be
established in each temple, etc.; and as a part of the
great plan to do honour to the king it was ordered that
a copy of the decree, inscribed on a basalt stele in
hieroglyphic, demotic, and Greek characters, should be
set up in each of the first, second, and third grade
temples near the king's statue. The provisions of this
decree were carried out in the eighth year of the king's
reign, and the Rosetta Stone is one of the stelae which,
presumably, were set up in the great temples throughout the length and breadth of the land. But the importance of the stone historically is very much less than
its value philologically, for the decipherment of the
Egyptian hieroglyphics is centred in it, and it formed
the base of the work done by scholars in the past
century which has resulted in the restoration of the
ancient Egyptian language and literature.

It will be remembered that long before the close of
the Roman rule in Egypt the hieroglyphic system of
writing had fallen into disuse, and that its place had
been taken by demotic, and by Coptic, that is to say,
the Egyptian language written in Greek letters; the
widespread use of Greek and Latin among the govern-

ing and upper classes of Egypt also caused the disappearance of Egyptian as the language of state. The study of hieroglyphics was prosecuted by the priests in remote districts probably until the end of the Vth century of our era, but very little later the ancient inscriptions had become absolutely a dead letter, and until the beginning of the last century there was neither an Oriental nor a European who could either read or understand a hieroglyphic inscription. Many writers pretended to have found the key to the hieroglyphics, and many more professed, with a shameless impudence which it is hard to understand in these days, to translate the contents of the texts into a modern tongue. Foremost among such pretenders must be mentioned Athanasius Kircher who, in the XVIIth century, declared that he had found the key to the hieroglyphic inscriptions ; the translations which he prints in his *Oedipus Aegyptiacus* are utter nonsense, but as they were put forth in a learned tongue many people at the time believed they were correct. More than half a century later the Comte de Pahlin stated that an inscription at Denderah was only a translation of Psalm C., and some later writers believed that the Egyptian inscriptions contained Bible phrases and Hebrew compositions.[1] In the first half of the XVIIIth century Warburton appears to have divined the existence of alphabetic characters in Egyptian, and had he pos-

[1] See my *Mummy*, p. 126.

sessed the necessary linguistic training it is quite possible that he would have done some useful work in
decipherment. Among those who worked on the right
lines must be mentioned de Guignes, who proved
the existence of groups of characters having determinatives, and Zoëga, who came to the conclusion that
the hieroglyphics were letters, and what was very
important, that the cartouches, *i. e.*, the ovals which
occur in the inscriptions and are so called because they
resemble cartridges, contained royal names.[1] In 1802
Akerblad, in a letter to Silvestre de Sacy, discussed
the demotic inscription on the Rosetta Stone, and published an alphabet of the characters. But Akerblad
never received the credit which was his due for this
work, for although it will be found, on comparing
Young's "Supposed Enchorial Alphabet" printed in 1818
with that of Akerblad printed in 1802, that *fourteen*
of the characters are identical in both alphabets, no
credit is given to him by Young. Further, if Champollion's alphabet, published in his *Lettre à M. Dacier*,
Paris, 1822, be compared with that of Akerblad, sixteen
of the characters will be found to be identical; yet
Champollion, like Young, seemed to be oblivious of the
fact.

With the work of Young and Champollion we reach
firm ground. A great deal has been written about the
merits of Young as a decipherer of the Egyptian hiero-

---

[1] *De Usu et Origine Obeliscorum*, Rome, 1797, p. 465.

glyphics, and he has been both over-praised and over-blamed. He was undoubtedly a very clever man and a great linguist, even though he lacked the special training in Coptic which his great rival Champollion possessed. In spite of this, however, he identified correctly the names of six gods, and those of Ptolemy and Berenice; he also made out the true meanings of several ideographs, the true values of six letters[1] of the alphabet, and the correct consonantal values of three[2] more. This he did some years before Champollion published his Egyptian alphabet, and as priority of publication (as the late Sir Henry Rawlinson found it necessary to say with reference to his own work on cuneiform decipherment) must be accepted as indicating priority of discovery, credit should be given to Young for at least this contribution towards the decipherment. No one who has taken the pains to read the literature on the subject will attempt to claim for Young that the value of his work was equal to that of Champollion, for the system of the latter scholar was eminently scientific, and his knowledge of Coptic was wonderful, considering the period when he lived. Besides this the quality of his hieroglyphic work was so good, and the amount of it which he did so great, that in those respects the two rivals ought not to be compared. He certainly knew of Young's results, and the admission by him

[1] *I. e.,* 𓇋𓇋 *i,* ⸺ *m,* 〰〰 *n,* ▢ *p,* ⤬⸺ *f,* ⌒ *l*

[2] *I. e.,* 𓂧, 𓄿, 𓏏.

that they existed would have satisfied Young's friends, and in no way diminished his own merit and glory.

In the year 1815 Mr. J. W. Bankes discovered on the Island of Philae a red granite obelisk and pedestal which were afterwards removed at his expense by G. Belzoni and set up at Kingston Hall in Dorsetshire. The obelisk is inscribed with one column of hieroglyphics on each side, and the pedestal with twenty-four lines of Greek. In 1822 Champollion published an account of this monument in the *Revue encyclopédique* for March, and discussed the hieroglyphic and Greek inscriptions upon it. The Greek inscription had reference to a petition of the priests of Philae made to Ptolemy, and his wife Kleopatra, and his sister also called Kleopatra, and these names of course occur in it. Champollion argued that if the hieroglyphic inscription has the same meaning as the Greek, these names must also occur in it. Now the only name found on the Rosetta Stone is that of Ptolemy which is, of course, contained in a cartouche, and when Champollion examined the hieroglyphic inscription on the Philae obelisk, he not only found the royal names there, enclosed in cartouches, but also that one of them was identical with that which he knew from the Greek of the Rosetta Stone to be that of Ptolemy. He was certain that this name was that of Ptolemy, because in the Demotic inscription on the Rosetta Stone the group of characters which formed the name occurred over and over again, and in the places where, according to the Greek, they ought

to occur. But on the Philae Obelisk the name Kleopatra is mentioned, and in both of the names of Ptolemy
and Kleopatra the same letters occur, that is to say L
and P; if we can identify the letter P we shall not only
have gained a letter, but be able to say at which end
of the cartouches the names begin. Now writing down
the names of Ptolemy and Kleopatra as they usually
occur in hieroglyphics we have :—

Ptolemy

Kleopatra

Let us however break the names up a little more
and arrange the letters under numbers thus :—

Ptolemy.

1. 2. 3. 4. 5. 6. 7.

Kleopatra.

1. 2. 3. 4. 5. 6. 7. 8. 9. 10. 11.

We must remember too that the Greek form of the
name Ptolemy is Ptolemaios. Now on looking at the
two names thus written we see at a glance that letter
No. 5 in one name and No. 1 in the other are identical,
and judging by their position only in the names they
must represent the letter P; we see too that letter No. 2

in one name and No. 4 in the other are also identical, and arguing as before from their position they must represent the letter L. We may now write down the names thus :—

P ⌒ 𝓈𝓁 L ⌒ 𝖰𝖰 𝗅

⊿ L 𝖨 𝓈𝓁 P 🦅 ⌒ ⌒ 🦅 ⌒ ○

As only one of the names begin with P, that which begins with that letter must be Ptolemy. Now letter No. 4 in one name, and letter No. 3 in the other are identical, and also judging by their position we may assign it in each name the value of some vowel sound like O, and thus get :—

P ⌒ O L ⌒ 𝖰𝖰 𝗅

⊿ L 𝖨 O P 🦅 ⌒ ⌒ 🦅 ⌒ ○

But the letter between P and O in Ptolemy must be T, and as the name ends in Greek with S, the last letter in hieroglyphics must be S, so we may now write down the names thus :—

P T O L ⌒ 𝖰𝖰 S

⊿ L 𝖨 O P 🦅 ⌒ ⌒ 🦅 T ○

Now if we look, as Champollion did, at the other ways in which the name of Kleopatra is written we shall find that instead of the letter ⟨⟩ we sometimes have the letter ⌒ which we already know to be T, and as in the Greek form of the name this letter has an A before it, we may assume that 🦅 = A; the initial letter must, of course, be K. We may now write the names thus :—

$$\text{P T O L} \underset{5.}{\;\text{⟨⟩}\;} \underset{6.}{\text{🮲🮲}} \text{S}$$

$$\underset{3.}{\text{K L 🮲}} \text{O P A T} \underset{8.}{\text{⟨⟩}} \text{A T} \underset{11.}{\text{⌒}}$$

The sign 🮲 (No. 3) in the name Kleopatra represents some vowel sound like E, and this sign doubled (No. 6) represents the vowels AI in the name Ptolemaios; but as 🮲🮲 represent EE, or Î, that is to say I pronounced in the Continental fashion, the O of the Greek form has no equivalent in hieroglyphics. That leaves us only the signs ⟨⟩, ⟨⟩ and ⌒ to find values for. Young had proved that the signs ⌒ᵒ always occurred at the ends of the names of goddesses, and that ⌒ᵒ was a feminine termination; as the Greek kings and queens of Egypt were honoured as deities, this termination was added to the names of royal ladies also. This disposes of the signs ⌒ᵒ, and the letters ⟨⟩ (No. 5) and ⟨⟩ (No. 8) can be nothing else but M and R. So we may now write :—

P T O L M I S, *i. e.*, Ptolemy,

K L E O P A T R A, *i. e.*, Kleopatra.

Now a common title of the Roman Emperors was

written   hieroglyphically ⌒ ⋂⋂ ⋂ ⌒ —•—. We
know that ⋂⋂ = I, ⋂ = S, and ⌒ = R ; and as ⌒
is used as a variant for the first sign in the name of
Kleopatra given above, ⌒ must be K also. The last
sign —•— is interchanged with ⋂, and we may thus
write under the hieroglyphics the values as follows:—

⌒   ⋂⋂   ⋂   ⌒   —•—
K   I   S   R   S

that is to say Καισαρος or Caesar. From the different
ways in which the name of Ptolemy is written we learn
that 𝕊 = U, and that ℮ has also the same value,
and that 🐦 has the same value as ⌒, i. e., M, is also
apparent. Now we may consider a common Greek name
which is written in hieroglyphics ⟮ ⋂ ⇶ ⋂⋂ △ 🐦 ⟯ ;
we may break it up thus :—

1. 2.   3.   4.   5. 6.   7.   8. 9.

that is to say Kαισαρος

Of these characters we have already identified Nos. 2,
3, 5, 7, 8 and 9, and from the two last we know that
we are dealing with the name of a royal lady. But
there is also another common Greek name which may
be written out in this form :—

1.   2.   3.   4.   5.   6.   7.   8.

and we see at a glance that the only letter that we

have not met with before is 〰. **Reading the values
of this last group of signs we get** E R (*or* L) K S
T R (*or* L) S, which can be nothing else but Eleks-
ntrs or "Alexander"; thus we find that 〰 = N. Now
substituting this value for sign No. 4 in the royal lady's
name given above we read . E R N I . A T; and as the
Greek text of the inscription in which this name occurs
mentions Berenike, we conclude at once that No. 1
sign 〗 = B, and that No. 6 sign △ = K. From other
Greek and Latin titles and names we may obtain the
values of many other letters and syllables, as will be
seen from the following :—

1. P.H.I.U.L.I.U.P.U (*or* UA).S., *i. e.*, Philip.

2. P.I.L.A.T.R.A., *i. e.*, Philotera.

3. BA.R.N.I.K.T., *i. e.*, Berenice.

4. A.R.R.S.N.A.T., *i. e.*, Arsinoë.

A.R.S.I.N.A.I., *i. e.*, Arsinoë.

5. T.R.A.P.N.T., *i. e.*, Tryphaena.

6. T.BA.R.I.S.K.I.S.R. S., *i. e.*, Tiberius Caesar.

7. K-A-I-S K-A-I-S-R-S K-R-M-

i. e., Gaius   Caesar   Germ-

NI-K-I-S

anicus.

8. K-L-UT-S   T-I-BA-R-SA

i. e., Claudius   Tiberius.

9. A-U-TU-K-R-T-R   K-I-S-R-S

i. e.,   Autocrator   Caesar.

T-A-T-A-S   A-R-I-S   A-T-R-I-N-S

Titus   Aelius   Hadrianus.

10. A-U-R-L   A-I-S   AN-TA-N-I-N-S

i. e.,   Aurelius   Antoninus.

In the Ptolemaic and Roman times the titles of the kings or emperors were often included in the cartouches, and from some of these Champollion derived a number of letters for his Egyptian alphabet. Thus many kings call themselves ⬛𝟾⌣, and ♀ ⌐, which appellations were known to mean "Of Ptah beloved" and "living ever". Now in the first of these ⬛𝟾⌣ we know, from the names which we have read above, that the first two signs are P and T, *i. e.*, the first two letters of the name Ptah; the third sign 𝟾 must then have the value of H or of some sound like it. If these three signs ⬛𝟾 form the name of Ptah, then the fourth sign ⌐ must mean "beloved". Now as Coptic is only a dialect of Egyptian written in Greek letters we may obtain some help from it as Champollion did; and as we find in that dialect that the ordinary words for "to love" are *mei* and *mere*, we may apply one or other of these values to the sign ⌐. In the same way, by comparing variant texts, it was found that ♀ was what is called an ideograph meaning "life", or "to live"; now the Coptic word for "life" or "to live", is *ônkh*, so the pronunciation of the hieroglyphic sign must be something like it. We find also that the variant spellings of ♀ give us ♀〰⬤, and as we already know that 〰 = N, the third sign ⬤ must be KH; incidentally, too, we discover that ♀ has the syllabic value of *ānkh*, and that the *ā* has become *ô* in Coptic. If, in the appellation ♀ ⌐, *i. e.*, "living ever", ♀ means "life", it is clear that ⌐ must mean "ever". Of the three signs which form the word we already know the last two, ⌢ and ⌐, for we have

seen the first in the name Ptolemy, and the second in
the name Antoninus, where they have the values of T
and TA respectively. Now it was found by comparing
certain words written in hieroglyphics with their equivalents in Coptic that the third sign ⌐⌐ was the equivalent of a letter in the Coptic alphabet which we may
transliterate by TCH, *i. e.*, the sound which *c* has before
i in Italian. Further investigations carried on in the
same way enabled Champollion and his followers to
deduce the syllabic values of the other signs, and at
length to compile a classified syllabary. We may now
collect the letters which we have gathered together
from the titles and names of the Greek and Roman
rulers of Egypt in a tabular form thus :—

𓅓 A		𓎡 H
𓏤 A *or* E		𓏞 H
𓈖 Ā		● KH
𓏭𓏭 *or* ⧵ I		—• *or* 𓏲 S
𓅿 *or* ⊙ *or* 𓎂 O *or* U		⌒ T
𓂉 B		𓏏 T
◻ P		⌐ T
𓅓 *or* ⌐ M		⌐⌐ TCH
⌁⌁⌁ *or* 𓈖 N		⌐ K
𓂝 *or* ⌐ R		◿ K
		𓂸 K

It will be noticed that we have three different kinds of the K sound, three of the T sound, two of the H sound, and three A sounds. At the early date when the values of the hieroglyphics were first recovered it was not possible to decide the exact difference between the varieties of sounds which these letters represented; but the reader will see from the alphabet on pp. 31, 32 the values which are generally assigned to them at the present time. It will be noticed, too, that among the letters of the Egyptian alphabet given above there are no equivalents for F and SH, but these will be found in the complete alphabet.

CHAPTER III.

HIEROGLYPHICS AS IDEOGRAPHS, PHONETICS, AND DETERMINATIVES.

Every hieroglyphic character is a picture of some object in nature, animate or inanimate, and in texts many of them are used in more than one way. The simplest use of hieroglyphics is, of course, as pictures, which we may see from the following :— a hare; an eagle; a duck; a beetle; a field with plants growing in it; ⋆ a star; a twisted rope; a comb; a pyramid, and so on. But hieroglyphics may also represent *ideas, e. g.,* a wall falling down sideways represents the idea of "falling"; a hall in which deliberations by wise men were made represents the idea of "counsel"; an axe represents the idea of a divine person or a god; a musical instrument represents the idea of pleasure, happiness, joy, goodness, and the like. Such are called **ideographs.** Now every picture of every object must have had a name, or we may say that each picture was a word-sign ; a list of all these arranged in proper order would have made a dictionary in the earliest times. But let us suppose that at the period when these pictures were used as pictures only in Egypt, or wherever they first appeared, the king wished to put on record that an embassy from some such and such a neighbouring potentate had visited him with such and such an object, and that the chief of the embassy, who was called by such and such a name, had brought him rich presents from his master. Now the scribes of the period could, no doubt, have reduced to writing an account of the visit, without any very great difficulty, but when they came to recording the name of the distinguished visitor, or that of his master, they would not find this to be an easy matter. To have written down the name they would be obliged to make use of a number of hieroglyphics or picture characters which represented most closely the sound of the name of the envoy, without the least regard to their meaning as pictures, and, for the moment, the picture characters would have represented sounds only. The scribes must have done the same had they been ordered to make a list of the presents which the envoy had brought for their royal master. Passing over the evident anachronism let us call the envoy "Ptolemy", which name we may write, as in the preceding chapter, with the signs :—

Now No. 1 represents a door, No. 2 a cake, No. 3 a

knotted rope, No. 4 a lion, No. 5 (uncertain), No. 6 two reeds, and No. 7 a chairback ; but here each of these characters is employed for the sake of its *sound* only.

The need for characters which could be employed to express *sounds only* caused the Egyptians at a very early date to set aside a considerable number of picture signs for this purpose, and to these the name of **phonetics** has been given. Phonetic signs may be either **syllabic** or **alphabetic**, *e. g.*, ◯ *peḥ*, ◯ *mut*, ◯ *maāt*, ◯ *χeper*, which are syllabic, and ◯ *p*, ◯ *b*, ◯ *m*, ◯ *r*, ◯ *k*, which are alphabetic. Now the five alphabetic signs just quoted represent as pictures, a door, a foot and leg, an owl, a mouth, and a vessel respectively, and each of these objects no doubt had a name ; but the question naturally arises how they came to represent single letters ? It seems that the sound of the *first letter* in the name of an object was given to the picture or character which represented it, and henceforward the character bore that phonetic value. Thus the first character ◯ P, represents a door made of a number of planks of wood upon which three cross-pieces are nailed. There is no word in Egyptian for door, at all events in common use, which begins with P, but, as in Hebrew, the word for door must be connected with the root "to open" ; now the Egyptian word for "to open" is ◯ *pt[a]ḥ*, and as we know that the first character in that word has the sound of P and of no other letter, we may reasonably assume that the Egyptian word for "door" began with P. The third

character ![owl] M represents the horned owl, the name
of which is preserved for us in the Coptic word *mûlotch*
(ⲙⲟⲩⲗⲟⲭ); the first letter of this word begins with
M, and therefore the phonetic value of ![owl] is M. In
the same way the other letters of the Egyptian alphabet
were derived, though it is not always possible to say
what the word-value of a character was originally. In
many cases it is not easy to find the word-values of an
alphabetic sign, even by reference to Coptic, a fact
which seems to indicate that the alphabetic characters
were developed from word-values so long ago that the
word-values themselves have passed out of the written
language. Already in the earliest dynastic inscriptions
known to us hieroglyphic characters are used as pictures, ideographs and phonetics side by side, which
proves that these distinctions must have been invented
in pre-dynastic times.

The Egyptian alphabet is as follows :—

![glyph]	A (א)	![glyph]	F	(ב)	
![glyph]	Ȧ (’)	![owl] or ![glyph]	M	(מ)	
![glyph]	Ā (ע)	~~~ or ![glyph]	N	(נ)	
![glyph] or \\	I (י)	![glyph] or ![glyph]	R and L	(ר, ל)	
![glyph] or ℮	U (ו)	![glyph]	H	(ה)	
![glyph]	B (ב)	![glyph]	Ḥ	(ח)	
![glyph]	P (פ)	![glyph]	KH (χ)	(Arab. خ)	

⟶	S	(ם)	⟁	Ḳ	(ג)
⌐	S	(שׁ)	⌐	T	(ה)
⊏⊐	SH (Ṡ)	(שׁ)	⊂⊐	Ṯ	(ט)
⊂⊐	K	(כ)	⎬,⊏⊐	TH (θ)	(ת)
◿	Q	(ק)	⌐	TCH (T')	(צ)

The Egyptian alphabet has a great deal in common
with the Hebrew and other Semitic dialects in respect
of the guttural and other letters, peculiar to Oriental
peoples, and therefore the Hebrew letters have been
added to shew what I believe to be the general values
of the alphabetic signs. It is hardly necessary to say
that differences of opinion exist among scholars as to
the method in which hieroglyphic characters should
be transcribed into Roman letters, but this is not to be
wondered at considering that the scientific study of
Egyptian is only about ninety years old, and that the
whole of the literature has not yet been published.

Some ideographs have more than one phonetic value,
in which case they are called **polyphones**; and many
ideographs representing entirely different objects have
similar values, in which case they are called homo-
phones.

As long as the Egyptians used picture writing pure
and simple their meaning was easily understood, but
when they began to spell their words with alphabetic
signs and syllabic values of picture signs, which had

no reference whatever to the original meaning of the signs, it was at once found necessary to indicate in some way the meaning and even sounds of many of the words so written; this they did by adding to them signs which are called **determinatives**. It is impossible to say when the Egyptians first began to add determinatives to their words, but all known hieroglyphic inscriptions not pre-dynastic contain them, and it seems as if they must have been the product of prehistoric times. They, however, occur less frequently in the texts of the earlier than of the later dynasties.

Determinatives may be divided into two groups; those which determine a single species, and those which determine a whole class. The following determinatives of classes should be carefully noted:—

Character	Determinative of	Character	Determinative of
1.	to call, beckon	6. or	god, divine being or thing
2.	man	7.	goddess
3.	to eat, think, speak, and of whatever is done with the mouth	8.	tree
		9.	plant, flower
		10. ꕔ, ꐢ	earth, land
4.	inertness, idleness	11.	road, to travel
5.	woman	12.	foreign land

Character	Determinative of	Character	Determinative of
13.	nome	26.	fish
14.	water	27.	rain, storm
15.	house	28.	day, time
16.	to cut, slay	29.	village, town, city
17.	fire, to cook, burn	30.	stone
18.	smell (good or bad)	31.	metal
19.	to overthrow	32.	grain
20.	strength	33.	wood
21.	to walk, stand, and of actions performed with the legs	34.	wind, air
		35.	foreigner
22.	flesh	36.	liquid, unguent
23.	animal	37.	abstract
24.	bird	38.	crowd, collection of people
25.	little, evil, bad	39.	children.

A few words have no determinative, and need none, because their meaning was fixed at a very early period, and it was thought unnecessary to add any ; examples of such are 〈image〉 *ḥenā*[1] "with", 〈image〉 *àm* "in", 〈image〉 *māk* "verily" and the like. On the other hand a large number of words have one determinative, and several have more than one. Of words of one determinative the following are examples :—

1. 〈image〉 *àm* to eat ; a picture of a man putting food into his mouth 〈image〉 is the determinative.

2. 〈image〉 *ānχ* a flower ; the picture of a flower 〈image〉 is the determinative.

3. 〈image〉 *sma* to slay ; the picture of a knife 〈image〉 is the determinative, and indicates that the word *sma* means "knife", or that it refers to some action that is done with a knife.

4. 〈image〉 *ses* bolt ; the picture of the branch of a tree 〈image〉 is the determinative, and indicates that *ses* is an object made of wood.

Of words of one or more determinatives the following are examples :—

1. 〈image〉 *renpit* flowers ; the pictures of a flower in the bud 〈image〉, and a flower 〈image〉, are the determinatives ; the three strokes I I I are the sign of the plural.

---

[1] Strictly speaking there is no *e* in Egyptian, and it is added in the transliterations of hieroglyphic words in this book simply to enable the reader to pronounce them more easily.

2.   *Ḥāp* god of the Nile ; the pictures of water enclosed by banks ▭, and running water 〰〰, and a god 𓀀 are the determinatives.

3.   *nemmeḫu* poor folk ; the pictures of a child 𓀔, and a man 𓀀, and a woman 𓀀 are the determinatives, and shew that the word *nemmeḫ* means a number of human beings, of both sexes, who are in the condition of helpless children.

Words may be spelt (1) with alphabetic characters wholly, or (2) with a mixture of alphabetic and syllabic characters ; examples of the first class are :—

	sfenṭ	a knife
	åsfet	wickedness
	šāt	a book
	uåa	a boat
	ḥeqer	to be hungry, hunger
	semeḫi	left hand side
	šešeš	a sistrum.

And examples of the second class are :—

1. [hieroglyphs] *ḥenkset* hair, in which [sign] has by itself the value of *ḥen*; so the word might be written [hieroglyphs] or [hieroglyphs]

2. [hieroglyphs] *neḥebet* neck, in which [sign] has by itself the value of *neḥ*; so the word might be written [hieroglyphs] as well as [hieroglyphs].

3. [hieroglyphs] *reχit* men and women, in which [sign] has by itself the value of *reχit*; thus in [hieroglyphs] the word is actually written twice, for [sign] = [hieroglyphs].

In many words the last letter of the value of a syllabic sign is often written in order to guide the reader as to its pronunciation. Take the word [hieroglyphs]. The ordinary value of [sign] is *mester* "car", but the [sign] which follows it shews that the sign is in this word to be read *mestem*, and the determinative indicates that the word means that which is smeared under the eye, or "eye-paint, stibium". For convenience' sake we may call such alphabetic helps to the reading of words **phonetic complements**. The following are additional examples, the phonetic complement being **marked by an asterisk**.

Hieroglyphs	Transliteration	Meaning
	mester	ear
	ḥai	rain
	šenār	storm
	merḫu	unguent
	ḥememu	mankind.

We may now take a short extract from the Tale of the Two Brothers, which will illustrate the use of alphabetic and syllabic characters and determinatives; the determinatives are marked by *, and the syllabic characters by †; the remaining signs are alphabetic. (N. B. There is no *e* in Egyptian.)

un	*ȧn*	*paif* His	*sen* brother	*āa* elder	*ḥer*

χeperu became	*mȧ* like	*ȧbu* panthers	*shematu* southern.	*ȧu-f* He	*ḥer*

ṭāt made	*ṭemtu* sharp	*paif* his	*nui* dagger,

àu-f	*ḥer*	*ṭātu-f*	*em*	*ṭet-f*	*un* *àn*
he		placed it	in	his hand.	

paif	*sen*	*āu*	*āḥā*	*en*
His	brother	elder	stood	

ḥa	*pa*	*sbai*	*paif*
behind	the	door	of his

àhait	*er*	*χaṭbu*	*paif*
stable	to	stab	his

sen	*seràu*	*em*	*paif*	*i*	*em*
brother	younger	at	his	coming	at

ruha	*er·*	*ṭāt*	*āq*	*naif*
eventide	to	make	to enter	his

àaut	*er*	*pa*	*àhait*
cattle	into	the	stables.

χer	àr	pa	Śu	her	ḥetep	àu-f

Now when the god Shu　　was setting　　he

her	atep-f	stimu	neb

was loading himself　with green herbs　of all kinds

en	seχet	em	paif	seχeru

of　the fields according　to his　habit

enti	hru	neb	àu-f	her	i	àu	ta

of　day　every,　he was coming [home].　The

aḥt	ḥauti	her	āq	er	pa

cow　leading　　entered　into　the

àhait	àu	set	her	teṭ	en

stable,　　she　　said　to

pai-set	saàu	mākuà	paik

her　keeper,　Verily　thy

sen	āa	aḥā	er	ḥāt-tuk	χeri
brother	elder	standeth		in front of thee	with

paif	nui	er	χaṭbu	- k
his	dagger	to	stab	thee;

ruȧ - k	tu	er - ḥāt - f	un	ȧn - f
run away		from before him.		He

ḥer	setem	pa	ṭeṭ	taif	ȧḥ
hearkened	unto	the	speech	of his	cow

ḥāuti	ȧu	ta	ket-θȧ	ḥer	āq
leading.		The next		entered, [and]

ȧu	set	ḥer	ṭeṭ - θȧ - f	em	mȧtet	ȧuf
	she was saying to him			likewise.	He

ḥer	ennu	χeri	pa	sba	en
looked	under	the		door	of

paif	àhait	àuf	her
his	stable,	he	

petrà	reṭ	en	paif
saw the legs		of	his

sen	āa	àuf	āḥā	en	ḥa
brother	elder	[as] he	stood		behind

pa	sba	àu	paif	nui
the	door		his	dagger

em	ṭet-f	àuf	her	uaḥ	taif
in his hand.		He		set	his

atep	er	pa	àuṭent	àuf	her
load	upon	the	ground,	he betook	

fa - f	er	seχseχ	θāu
himself	to	flight	rapid.

CHAPTER IV.[1]

A SELECTION OF HIEROGLYPHIC CHARACTERS WITH THEIR PHONETIC VALUES, ETC.

1. FIGURES OF MEN.

		Phonetic value.	Meaning as ideograph or determinative.
1.		*enen*	man standing with inactive arms and hands, submission
2.		*å*	to call, to invoke
3.		*kes* (?)	man in beseeching attitude, propitiation
5.		*ṭua* ⎫	
6.		*ṭua* ⎭	to pray, to praise, to adore, to entreat
7.		*hen*	to praise
8.		*qa, ḥāā*	to be high, to rejoice
9.		*ān*	man motioning something to go back, to retreat

[1] The numbers and classification of characters are those given by Herr Adolf Holzhausen in his *Hieroglyphen.*

10.		*ȧn*	man calling after someone, to beck-on
11.		*ȧn*	
12.		—	see No. 7
13.		—	see No. 10
14.			man hailing some one
15.		*ȧb*	to dance
16.		*ȧb*	to dance
17.		*ȧb*	to dance
18.		*ȧb*	to dance
19.		*kes*	man bowing, to pay homage
20.		*kes*	man bowing, to pay homage
21.		—	man running and stretching forward to reach something
22.		*sati*	to pour out water, to micturate
23.			
24.		*ḥeter*	two men grasping hands, friendship
25.		*ȧmen*	a man turning his back, to hide, to conceal

26.	nem	pygmy
27.	tut, sāḥu, qeres	image, figure, statue, mummy, transformed dead body
28.	tetta	a dead body in the fold of a serpent
29.	ur, ser	great, great man, prince, chief
30.	åau, ten	man leaning on a staff, aged
31.	neχt	man about to strike with a stick, strength
32.	—	man stripping a branch
33.	ṭua	. . . .
34.	seḥer	to drive away
35.	χeχeθ (?)	two men performing a ceremony (?)
36.	ŝema (?)	. . . .
37.	åḥi	man holding an instrument
38.	—	man holding an instrument
39.	—	man about to perform a ceremony with two instruments
40.	neχt	see No. 31
41.	—	to play a harp

42.		—	to plough
43.		ṭā	to give a loaf of bread, to give
44.		sa	to make an offering
45.		nini	man performing an act of worship
46.		āb	man throwing water over himself, a priest
47.		sati, set	man sprinkling water, purity
48.		—	a man skipping with a rope
49.		χus	man building a wall, to build
50.		—	man using a borer, to drill
51.		qeṭ	to build
52.		fa, kat	a man with a load on his head, to bear, to carry, work
53.		āχ	man supporting the whole sky, to stretch out
54.		fa	to bear, to carry ; see No. 52
55.		χesṭeb	man holding a pig by the tail......
56.		qes ⎞	to bind together, to force something
57.		qes ⎠	together
58.		ḥeq	man holding the ⎛ ḥeq sceptre, prince, king

59.	—	prince, king
62.	—	prince or king wearing White crown
63.	—	prince or king wearing Red crown
65.	—	prince or king wearing White and Red crowns
68.	*ur*	
69.	*ur*	great man, prince
70.	*àθi*	prince, king
71.	*ḥen*	a baby sucking its finger, child, young person
72.	*ḥen*	a child
74.	*ḥen*	a child wearing the Red crown
75.	*ḥen*	a child wearing the disk and uraeus
76.	*mesṭem*	. . . .
78.		
79.	*χefti*	a man breaking in his head with an axe or stick, enemy, death, the dead
80.		
82.	*māsā*	man armed with a bow and arrows, bowman, soldier
83.	*menf*	man armed with shield and sword, bowman, soldier

84.	—	man with his hands tied behind him, captive
85.	—	man with his hands tied behind him, captive
86.	—	man tied to a stake, captive
87.	—	man tied by his neck to a stake
88.	—	beheaded man tied by his neck to a stake
89.	sa, remt	man kneeling on one knee
90.	å	to cry out to, to invoke
91.	å	man with his right hand to his mouth, determinative of all that is done with the mouth
92.	enen	submission, inactivity
93.	hen	to praise
94.	ṭua	to pray, to praise, to adore, to entreat
96.	åmen	to hide
97.	—	to play a harp
98.	åuḥ, sur	to give or offer a vessel of water to a god or man
99.	sa	to make an offering
100.	åmen, ḥab	man hiding himself, to hide, hidden
101.	ab	man washing, clean, pure, priest

102.			
103		*āb*	man washing, clean, pure, priest
104.			

105.   *fa, kat*   man carrying a load; see No. 52

106.   *heḥ*   man wearing emblem of year, a large, indefinite number

107.   *heḥ*   a god wearing the sun's disk and grasping a palm branch in each hand

108.   —   to write

110.   —   dead person who has obtained power in the next world

111.   —   dead person, holy being

112.   —   dead person, holy being

113.   —   a sacred or divine person

114.   —   a sacred or divine king

115.   —   divine or sacred being holding the sceptre

116.   —   divine or sacred being holding the sceptre

117.   —   divine or sacred being holding the whip or flail

119.   —   divine or sacred being holding and

120.		—	king wearing the White crown and holding 𓏤 and 𓌙
121.		—	king wearing the Red crown and holding 𓏤 and 𓌙
123.		—	king wearing the Red and White crowns and holding 𓏤
124.		—	king wearing the Red and White crowns and holding 𓏤
125.		—	ibis-headed being, Thoth
126.		*sa*	a sacred person holding a cord? a guardian?
127.		*sa*	a sacred person holding a cord? a guardian?
128.		*sa*	a watchman, to guard, to watch
129.		—	a sacred person, living or dead
130.		—	
131.		*šeps*	a sacred person
132.		*netem*	a person sitting in state
133.		*χer*	to fall down
134.		*mit*	a dead person
135.		*meḥ*	to swim
136.		*neb*	a man swimming, to swim
137.			

2. Figures of Women

1.	ḥeter	two women grasping hands, friendship
3.	θehem	woman beating a tambourine, to rejoice
4.	ḳeb	to bend, to bow
5.	Nut	the goddess Nut, *i. e.*, the sky
6.	—	woman with dishevelled hair
7.	sat (?)	a woman seated
8.	—	a sacred being, sacred statue
9.	—	
10.	—	a divine or holy female, or statue
11.	—	
12.	ȧri	a guardian, watchman
13.	θehem	see No. 3
14.	beḳ	a pregnant woman
15.	mes, *pāpā*	a parturient woman, to give birth
16.	menā	to nurse, to suckle a child
17.	renen	to dandle a child in the arms

3. Figures of Gods and Goddesses.

1.   *Ausár* (or *Asár*) the god Osiris

3.   *Ptah*   the god Ptah

4.   *Ptah*   Ptah holding a sceptre, and wearing a *menát*

6.   *Ta-tunen*   the god Ta-tunen

7.   *Tanen*   the god Tanen

8.   *Ptah-Tanen* the god Ptah-Tanen

9.   *An-heru*   the god An-heru

10.   *Amen*   Ámen, or Menu, or Ámsu in his ithyphallic form.

11.   *Amen*   Ámen wearing plumes and holding

13.   *Amen*   Ámen wearing plumes and holding Maát

14.   *Amen*   Ámen wearing plumes and holding a short, curved sword

15.   *Amen*   Ámen holding the *user* sceptre

16.   *Aáh*   the Moon-god

17.   *xensu*   the god Khensu

18.   *Śu*   the god Shu

19.		*Śu*	the god Shu
20.		*Rā-usr-Maāt*	god Rā as the mighty one of Maāt
21.		*Ra*	the god Rā wearing the white crown
22.		*Ra*	Rā holding sceptres of the horizons of the east and west
23.		*Ra*	Rā holding the sceptre
24.		*Ra*	Rā wearing disk and uraeus and holding
25.		*Ra*	Rā wearing disk and uraeus
26.		*Ḥeru*	Horus (*or* Rā) wearing White and Red crowns
27.		*Ra*	Rā wearing disk and holding symbol of "life"
29.		*Ra*	Rā wearing disk, uraeus and plumes, and holding sceptre
31.		*Set*	the god Set
32.		*Anpu*	the god Anubis
33.		*Teḥuti*	the god Thoth
36.			
37.		*Xnemu*	the god Khnemu
38.			
39.		*Ḥāpi*	the Nile-god

40.		*Auset* (or *Ast*)	Isis holding papyrus sceptre
41.		*Auset* (or *Ast*)	Isis holding symbol of "life"
42.		*Auset* (or *Ast*)	Isis holding papyrus sceptre
45.		*Nebt-ḥet*	Nephthys holding symbol of "life"
51.		*Nut*	the goddess Nut
52.		*Seśeta*	the goddess Sesheta
53.		*Usr-Maāt*	the goddess Maāt with sceptre of strength
54. 55.		*Maāt*	the goddess Maāt
58.		*Ānqet*	the goddess Ānqet
62.		*Bast*	the goddess Bast
63.		*Seχet*	the goddess Sekhet
64. 65.		*Un*	the hare-god Un
66.		*Meḥit*	the goddess Meḥit
67.		*Śeta*	a deity
68.		*Seḥer*	a god who frightens, terrifies, or drives away

69.			
70.		*Seḫer*	see No. 68
71.		*Bes*	the god Bes
73.			
74.		*ẕeperả*	the god Khepera

4. MEMBERS OF THE BODY.

1.		*ṭep, tafa*	the head, the top of anything
3.		*ḥer, ḥrả*	the face, upon
5, 6, 7.		*šent, user*	the hair, to want, to lack
8.		*šere (?)*	a lock of hair
9.		*ẕabes*	the beard
10.		*mer, maa, ảri*	the right eye, to see, to look after something, to do
11.		—	the left eye
12.		*maa*	to see
13.		—	an eye with a line of stibium below the lower eye-lid
14.		*rem*	an eye weeping, to cry
15.		*an*	to have a fine appearance

16.		*merti, maa*	the two eyes, to see
17.		*uŧat*	the right eye of Rā, the Sun
18.		*uŧat*	the left eye of Rā, the Moon
19.		*uŧatti*	the two eyes of Rā
20.		*ŧebḫ*	an *utchat* in a vase, offerings
23.	o	*ȧr*	the pupil of the eye
24.		*ŧebḫ*	two eyes in a vase, offerings
25.		*ȧm*	eyebrow
26.		*mester*	ear
28.		*χent*	nose, what is in front
29.		*re*	opening, mouth, door
30.		*septi*	the two lips
31.		*sept*	lip raised shewing the teeth
32.		*ārt*	jawbone with teeth
33.	,	*tef, ȧŧet*	exudation, moisture
35, 36.	ǀ, ǀ	*meŧ*	a weapon or tool
37.		*ȧat, peṣ*	the backbone

38.	śaṭ	the chine
39.	menā	the breast
40, 41. 44.	seχen	to embrace
42. 47.	ȧn, ȧm	not having, to be without, negation
46.	ka	the breast and arms of a man, the double
49. 50.	ser, ṭeser	hands grasping a sacred staff, something holy
51.	χen	hands grasping a paddle, to transport, to carry away
52.	āḥa	arms holding shield and club, to fight
54.	uṭen	to write
58.	χu	hand holding a whip or flail, to be strong, to reign
59.	ā, ṭā	hand and arm outstretched, to give
62.	meḥ, ermen	to bear, to carry
63.	ṭā	to give
65.	mā	to give

66.   *mā, ḥenk*   to offer

67.   —   to offer fruit

68.   *nini*   an act of homage

69.   *neχt*   to be strong, to shew strength

72.   *χerp*   to direct

73, 76.   ,   *ṭet*   hand

74.   *šep*   to receive

77.   *kep*   to hold in the hand

82.   *am*   to clasp, to hold tight in the fist

84, 85.   *tebā*   finger, the number 10,000

—   *meter, āq*   to be in the centre, to give evidence

86.   *ān*   thumb

87.

88.   *maā*   a graving tool

90.   *baḥ, met, tai, ka*   phallus, what is masculine, husband, bull

91.   *utet*   to beget

92, 93.   ,   *sem, seshem*

94	⟁	*χerui*	male organs
95.	⊌	*ḥem*	woman, female organ
96.	⋀	*i*	to go, to walk, to stand
98.	⋀	*ān, ḥem*	to go backwards, to retreat
99.	⟋	*uār, ret, ment*	to flee, to run away
100.	⋩	*teḥa*	to invade, to attack
101.	⟈	*ḳer*	to hold, to possess
102.	◿	*q*	a knee
103.	⌡	*b*	a leg and foot
105.	⊣⊓	*āb*	arm + hand + leg
106.	⊏	*ṭeb*	hand + leg
107.	⥽	*āb*	horn + leg
109.	ℓ		
111.	ℓ	*ḥā*	piece of flesh, limb

5. Animals.

| 1. | 🐎 | *sesem* | horse |
| 2. | 🐎 | *nefer* | |

3.		*àḥ, ka*	ox
6.		*kaut*	cow
13.		*bà*	calf
14.		*àu*	calt
15.		*ba*	ram
16.		*ba*	Nubian ram of Åmen
17.		*àr*	oryx
19.		*sàḥ*	oryx, the transformed body, the spiritual body
22.		*χen*	a water bag
23.		*àa*	donkey
24.		*uher* (?)	dog
25.		*àmhet*	ape
29.		—	the ape of Thoth
31.		—	ape wearing Red crown
32.		—	ape bearing *utchat* or Eye of the sun
36.		*ma,* or *màau*	lion
38.		*l, r, ru, re*	lion couchant

43. χerefu, akeru   the lions of Yesterday and To-day

44. neb   . . . . . .

47. màu   cat

49. sab   jackal, wise person

52. —   the god Anubis, the god Áp-uat

55. seśeta   . . . .

56. χeχ   a mythical animal

57. —   wild boar

58. un   a hare

59. ab   elephant

61. àpt   hippopotamus

62. χeb   rhinoceros

63. rer   pig

65. ser   giraffe

66. set   the god Set, what is bad, death, etc.

68. set   the god Set

69. pennu   rat

5. Members of Animals

3.	![sign]	*åḥ*	ox
4, 5.	![sign]	*χent*	nose, what is in front
6.	![sign]	*χeχ*	head and neck of an ox
8.	![sign]	*śefit*	strength
9.	![sign]	—	head and neck of a ram
12.	![sign]	*śesa*	to be wise
14.	![sign]	*peḥ*	head and neck of a lion, strength
	![sign]	*peḥti*	two-fold strength
16.	![sign]	*ḥā*	head and paw of lion, the fore-part of anything, beginning
21.	![sign]		
22.	![sign]	*set*	. . . .
24.	![sign]		
30.	![sign]	*at*	hour, season
33.	![sign]	*åp*	the top of anything, the forepart
35.	![sign]	*åat*	rank, dignity
37.	![sign]	*åpt renpet*	opening of the year, the new year

41.	$\bar{a}b$	horn, what is in front
44.	$\dot{a}be\hbar$	tooth
45.	$\dot{a}be\hbar$	tooth
46.	$\dot{a}ten, mes\underline{\imath}er$	to do the duty of someone, vicar, ear, to hear
47.	$pe\hbar$	to attain to, to end
49.	$\chi epe\underline{s}$	thigh
51.		
52.	$nem, u\hbar em$	leg of an animal, to repeat
54.	kep	paw of an animal
55, 56.	. . . .	skin of an animal
57.		skin of an animal, animal of any kind
59.	. . . .	
60.	sat	an arrow transfixing a skin, to hunt
63.	$u\bar{a}, \dot{a}u\bar{a}, \dot{a}su$	bone and flesh, heir, progeny

7. Birds.

1.		*a*	eagle
2.		*maa*	eagle + sickle
3.		*ma*	eagle + ⊂▭
4.			
6.		*ti, neḥ*	a bird of the eagle class ?
7.			
8.		*Ḥeru*	hawk, the god Horus, god
9.		*bak*	hawk with whip or flail
10.		*Ḥerui*	the two Horus gods
11.		*Ḥeru*	Horus with disk and uraeus
12.		*Ḥeru*	Horus wearing the White and Red crowns
13.		*Ḥeru nub*	the "golden Horus"
15.		*neter*	god, divine being, king
16.		*ȧment*	the west
21.		*Ḥeru sma taui*	"Horus the uniter of the two lands"
22.		*Ḥeru Sept*	Horus-Sept

24.	χu	. . . .
28.	āχem, āṡem	sacred form or image
29.	Ḥeru-ṡuti	Horus of the two plumes
30.	mut, ner	vulture
33.	Nebti	the vulture crown and th uraeus crown
36, 43.	m	owl
38.		
39.	māʾ	to give
40.		
41.	mer	
42.	embaḥ	before
45.	teḥuti	ibis
46.	qem	to find
47.	ḥam	to snare, to hunt
48, 51.	Teḥuti	the god Thoth
53.	ba	the heart-soul
54.	baiu	souls

55.		*bak*	**to** toil, to labour
58.		*χu*	the spirit-soul
60.		*bennu*	a bird identified with the phoenix
61.		*bāḥ*	to flood, to inundate
63.		*uśa*	to make fat
64.		*ṭeśer*	red
65.		*tefa*	bread, cake, food
66.			
67.		*sa*	goose, son
69.		*tefa* (?)	food
70.		*seṭ*	to make to shake with fear, to tremble
71.		*āq*	duck, to go in
72.		*ḥetem*	to destroy
73.		*pa*	to fly
75.		*χen*	to hover, to alight
77.		*qema*, θ*en*	to make, to lift up, to distinguish
78.		*ṭeb*	. . . .

79.		*ur*	swallow, great
80.		*śeráu*	sparrow, little
81.		*ti*	a bird of the eagle kind
82.		*reχit*	intelligent person, mankind
83.		*u*	chicken
87.		*ta*	. . . .
88.			
		seš	birds' nest
90.			
91.		*śenţ*	dead bird, fear, terror
92.		*ba*	soul

8. Parts of Birds.

1.		*sa, apţ*	goose, feathered fowl
3.		*ner*	head of vulture
4.		*peḳ*	. . . .
8.		*χu*	head of the *bennu* bird
9.		*reχ*	. . . .
10.		*ámaχ*	eye of a hawk

11.   *ṭenḫ*   wing, to fly

13.   *śu, maā*   feather, what is right and true

17.   *ermen*   to bear, carry

18.   *śa*   foot of a bird

20.   —   to cut, to engrave

21.   *śa*   son, with ⌒ *t* daughter

9. Amphibious Animals.

1.   *śet*   turtle, evil, bad

2.   *āś*   lizard, abundance

4.   *at, seqa*   crocodile, to gather together

     áθi, ḫenti   prince

5, 6.   *at*   crocodile

7.   *Sebek*   the god Sebek

8.   *qam*   crocodile skin, black

9.   *Ḥeqt*   the goddess Ḥeqt

10.   *ḥefen*   young frog, 100,000

11.   *ārā*   serpent, goddess

16.

14. *Meḥent* the goddess Meḥent

15.

19. *ȧtur* shrine of a serpent goddess

22. *ḥef, fenṭ* worm

24. *Āpep* the adversary of Rā, Apophis

25. *t, ṭet* serpent, body

27. *met* . . . .

30. *f* a cerastes, asp

31. *sef* . . . .

32. *per* to come forth

33. *āq* to enter in

37. *ptaḥ* to break open

10. Fish.

1. *ȧn* fish

3. *betu* fish

6. *sepa* centipede

9. *nār* . . . . .

10.	𓆛	*χa*	dead fish or thing
11.	𓆟	} *bes*	to transport
12.	𓆞		
14.	𓆝	*χept*	thigh (?)

11. Insects.

1.	𓆤	*net, bȧt*	bee
3.	𓆥	*suten net* (or *bȧt*)	"King of the South and North"
4.	𓆣	*χeper*	to roll, to become, to come into being
7.	𓆱	*ȧf*	fly
8.	𓆗	*seneḥem*	grasshopper
9.	𓆲	*serq*	scorpion

12. Trees and Plants.

1, 2.	𓎛, 𓈙	*ȧm*	tree, what is pleasant
6.	𓆸	*bener*	palm tree
7.	𓆭	. . . .	acacia
9.	𓆱	*χet*	branch of a tree, wood

13, 14. ⌠, ⌡ ⌉
⌡ *renp, ter* shoot, young twig, year
15, 16, 17. ⌠, ⌡, ⌡ ⌋

18. ⌠ — eternal year

19. ⌠ — time

20, 21. △, ◁ *sept* a thorn

22. ⊥ *neχeb* shoot, name of a goddess and city

⊥⊥ *enen* —

24. ⊥ *su, suten* king of the South

25, 27. ⊥, ⊥ *shemā* south, name of a class of priestess

26. ⊥ *res,* south

28, 29. ⊥, ⊥ ⌉
⌡ *res* south
30, 31. ⊥, ⊥ ⌋

33. ⌠ *ȧ* feather

⌠⌠ *i* —

34. ⌠ *i* to go

35. ▥▥▥ *seχet* plants growing in a field

36. ▨ *āb* an offering

37. 𓆟 } *šā, akh* lotus and papyrus flowers growing,
38. 𓆟   field

40. 𓎛 *ḥen* cluster of flowers or plants

42, 43. 𓆼, 𓆽 *ḥa* cluster of lotus flowers

44. 𓆸 *meḥt* the North, the Delta country, the land of the lotus

45. 𓆸 } *res* the South, the papyrus country
46. 𓆸

47. 𓇅 } *uat* young plant, what is green
48. 𓇉

55. 𓆰 — flower

58. 𓈖 *neḥem* flower bud

62. 𓆼 } — lotus flower
63. 𓆽

67. 𓊽 *un* . . . . .

68. 𓆷 *χa* flower

70. 𓆸 *šen* . . . .

73, 77. 𓆷, ◊ *ut, ut* to give commands

74, 75.   *ḥet*   white, shining, light

78.   *χesef*   an instrument, to turn back

80.   *mes*   to give birth

81.   —   the union of the South and North

82.   *beti*   barley

83.

86.   —   grain

88.   *šen*   granary, barn, storehouse

89.

90.   *årp*   grapes growing, wine

91.

92.   *mår*   pomegranate

93, 94.   *bener*   sweet, pleasant

96.

98.   *netem*   sweet, pleasant

13. Heaven, Earth and Water.

1. ▭	*pet, her*	what is above, heaven
2.		
3.	} *kerh*	sky with a star or lamp, night
4.	*átet*	water falling from the sky, dew, rain
5.	*Oehen*	lightning
6. ▭	*qert*	one half of heaven
7. ☉	*Rā, hru*	the Sun-god, day
9. ☼	*χu*	radiance
10, 11.	*Ra*	the Sun-god
13.	*χu, uben*	the sun sending forth rays, splendour
14. △	*Sept*	the star Sothis, to be provided with
16.	—	the sun's disk with uraci
17.	—	winged disk
23, 25.	*χā*	the rising sun
26. ⊖	*paut*	cake, offering, ennead of gods
28.	*sper*	a rib, to arrive at

29. ⌣ *áâḫ, âbṭ* moon, month

35. ★ *sba, ṭua* star, star of dawn, hour, to pray

36. ⊗ *ṭuat* the underworld

37. ▭ ⎫
       ⎬ *ta* land
38. ▭ ⎭

40. ⌒⌒ *set* (or *sent*) mountainous land

41. ⌒ — foreign, barbarian

42. ⌒ *ṭu* mountain, wickedness

44. ⌒ *χut* horizon

45, 46. ▦, ▤ *ḥesp, sept* nome

47. ▽ *áṭeb* the land on one side of the Nile ;
                ▽▽ = all Egypt

48. ⊠ — land

49. ⚏ *uat, ḥer* a road, a way

50. ⊂ *ḳes, m* side

51, 52. ▭, ▥ *áner* stone

53. • *šā* (?) sand, grain, fruit, nuts

55. ∿ *n* surface of water, water

	∿∿∿∿	*mu*	water
57. 58.		*mer*	ditch, watercourse, to love
60.		*sha*	lake
61.		*śem*	to go
62.		—	lake
64.		*Amen*	the god Amen
66.		*ḋa*	island
68.		*χuti*	the two horizons (*i. e.*, East and West)
69.		*peḥ*	swamp, marsh
70. 71. 72.		*ḥemt, bảa*	metal, iron ore (*or* copper ore?)

14. Buildings.

1.	⊗	*nu*	town, city
3.		*per*	house, to go out
6.		*per-χeru*	sepulchral meals or offerings

7.	⊹	*per ḥet*	"white house", treasury
8.		*h*	
10.		*mer*	quarter of a city (?)
11, 12.	,	*ḥet*	house, temple
13.		*ḥetu*	temples, sanctuaries
14.		*neter ḥet*	god's house
16.		*ḥet āa*	great house
17.		*Nebt-ḥet*	Lady of the house, *i. e.*, Nephthys
19.		*Ḥet-Ḥeru*	House of Horus, *i. e.*, Hathor
29.		*āḥā*	great house, palace
32.		*useχt*	hall, courtyard
36.		*ȧneb, sebti*	wall, fort
37.		*uhen*	to overthrow
41.		—	fortified town
43.			
44.		*seb*	door, gate
45.		*qenb*	corner, an official

48.	⌐▌	ḥap	to hide
51, 52.	△, ◺ —		pyramid
53.	▮	teχen	obelisk
54.	⋂	utu	memorial tablet
55.	⋂	uχa	pillar
61.	⋀	χaker	a design or pattern
62.	⋒	seḥ, ārq	a hall, council-chamber
64.	⋓	seṭ ḥeb (?)	festival celebrated every thirty years
65.	⊡	ḥeb	festival
67.	◿		double staircase, to go up
68.	◿	χet	staircase, to go up
69.	▭	āa	leaf of a door, to open
70.	—⊷	s	a bolt, to close
71.	⊐⊐	ås, seb, mes	to bring, to bring quickly
72, 73.	▷◁, ▷—◁	θes	to tie in a knot
74.	◁□▷	åmes	. . . .
75.	⊤	Åmsu	the god Amsu (or Min ?)
76.	▯	qeṭ	. . . .

15. Ships and parts of Ships.

1.			
2.		*uȧa, χeṭ*	boat, to sail down stream

5, 6.   *uḥā*   loaded boat, to transport

14.   —   to sail up stream

16.   *nef, ṭau*   wind, breeze, air, breath

19.   *āḥā*   to stand

21.   *ḥem*   helm, rudder

22.   *χeru*   paddle, voice

23.   *seŝep*   . . . .

61.   *ḥennu*   the name of a sacred boat

62.		
63.	—	boats of the sun

16. Seats, Tables, etc.

1.   *ȧst, Ȧuset*   seat, throne, the goddess Isis

2.   *ḥet*   . . . . . .

3.   —   seat, throne

5, 6.	𓄤, 𓄥	*ås*	. . . .
7.			to lie down in sleep or death
8.		*ster*	
9.		*s*	. . . . . .
11.		*sem, seśem*	. . . .
12.		—	clothes, linen
15.		*serer*	. . . . . .
16.		*ḥetep*	table of offerings
19.		*χer*	what is under, beneath
20, 22.			
23, 24.		—	funeral chest, sarcophagus
25.		*åat*	zone, district
27.		*ṭeb*	to provide with
28, 29.		*ån*	pillar, light tower (?)
30.		*ḥen*	. . . .
31, 33.		*ås*	. . . .
36.			squeezing juice from grapes,
37.		*nem*	the god Shesmu or Seshmu

38. 𓎼 ⎫
        meter   to use violence
39. ⎭

41. *šes* — linen, clothing, garments

43. *urš* — pillow

44. *un-ḥrȧ* — mirror

45, 46. *serit, χaibit* — fan, shadow

47. *māχa* — scales, to weigh

50. ⎫
        utȧ   to balance, to test by weighing
51. ⎭

52, 53, 54. ⎫
        uθes, res to raise up, to wake up
55. ⎭

57. *maāt* — a reed whistle, what is right or straight

58. *ȧat* — standard

17. TEMPLE FURNITURE.

2. *χaut* — altar

4. — — fire standard

13. *neter* — axe or some instrument used in the performance of magical ceremonies

16.		*neter χert*	the underworld
18.		*ṭeṭ*	the tree-trunk that held the dead body of Osiris, stability
20.		*sma*	to unite
22.		*sen*	brother
23.		*śen*	. . . .
26.		*ȧb*	the left side
28.		*ȧm*	to be in
29.		*Seśeta*	name of a goddess

18. CLOTHING, ETC.

1.		*meḥ*	head-gear
7.		*χeperś*	helmet
8.		*ḥeṭ*	the White crown of the South
9.		*res*	the South land
11.		*ṭeśer*	the Red crown of the North
12.		*meḥt*	the North land
13.		*seχeṭ*	the White and Red crowns united
14.		*u, śaā*	cord, one hundred

17.		*śuti*	two feathers
18.			
20.		*atef*	plumes, disk and horns
24.		*meḥ*	crown, tiara
25.			
26.		*useχ*	breast plate
28.		*àāḥ*	collar
29.		*sat*	garment of network
30.		*śent*	tunic
32.		*ḥebs*	linen, garments, apparel
34.		*mesen*	
36.		*mer, nes*	tongue, director
38.		*tebt*	sandal
39.		*śen, χetem*	circle, ring
41.		*ṭemt, temṭ*	to collect, to join together
42.		*θet*	buckle
43.		*anχ*	life

45.		sefaut	a seal and cord
46.		menåt	an instrument worn and carried by deities and men
47.		kep	. . . . . .
48.		åper	to be equipped
50.		χerp	to direct, to govern
52.		seχem	to be strong, to gain the mastery
56.		åment	the right side
59.			
60.		χu	fly-flapper
61.		Abt	the emblem containing the head of Osiris worshipped at Abydos
62.		ḥeq	sceptre, to rule
64.		tchåm	sceptre
65.		Uast	Thebes
66.		usr	strength, to be strong
73.		åmes	name of a sceptre
74.		χu	flail or whip
76.		Beb	the firstborn son of Osiris
77.		seχer	fringe (?)

19. ARMS AND ARMOUR.

1.	⟩	*āam, neḥes, qema, tebā*	foreign person, to make, finger
	⟩⟩	*āq*	what is opposite, middle
3.	⟩	*āb*	. . . .
	⟩	*seṭeb, seṭeb*	what is hostile
7, 8.	⟩, ⟲	*qeḥ*	axe
9.	⟩	*ṭep*	the first, the beginning
10.	⟩	*χepeš*	scimitar
11.	⌣	*χaut*	knife
12.	⌐	*k*	knife
13.	⟨	*qeṭ*	dagger
14, 15.	⟍, ⌐	*ṭes*	knife
19.	⌂	*nemmet*	block of slaughter
20.	⟍	*sešem*	. . . .
21.	⌣	*pet*	bow
25.	ﬤ		
		sta, or *sti*	the front of any thing
26.	ﬤ		

28.		*peṭ*	to stretch out, to extend
33.		*set*	arrow, to shoot
38.		*sa*	the side or back
41.		*āa*	great
42.		*sun*	arrow
43.		*χa*	body
45.		} *urit*	chariot
46.			

20. Tools, etc.

1.		*m*	, ...
2.		*tåt*	emanation
3.		*setep*	to select, to choose
4.		} *en*	adze
5.			
7.		*ḥu*	to fight, to smite
8.		*ma*	sickle
9.		*maå*	sickle cutting a reed (?)

12.		*mer, ḥen*	to love
13.		*heb, ār, per*	to plough, hall, growing things
14.		*tem*	to make perfect, the god Temu
15.		*bàt*	miraculous, wonderful
18.		*sa*	. . . .
19.		*θ*	. . . .
20.		—	metal
21.		*ta*	fire-stick (?)
26.		*menχ*	good, to perform
28.		*ḥemt*	workman
29.		*āba*	to open out a way
31.		*ab, (àb, āb,) mer*	disease, death
35.		*neṭ*	to break
38.		*uā*	one
40.		*Net*	the goddess Neith
42.		*šes, šems*	to follow after, follower
45.		*qes*	bone

No.	Sign	Transliteration	Meaning
47.		*seḥ*	estate, farm
48.			
49.		*ḥep*	to hide away
50.		*nub*	gold
53.		*ḥet*	silver
54.		*uasm, smu*	refined copper
55.		*seχet*	fowler's net

21. CORDWORK, NETWORK.

No.	Sign	Transliteration	Meaning
1.		*u, šaā*	cord, one hundred
2.		*sta*	to pull, to haul along
5.		*ȧn*	to be long, extended
		ȧmaχ	pious, sacred
6.		*šes, qes, qeb*	to fetter, linen bandage
8.			
9, 10.		—	to unfasten, book, writing
13.		*ārq*	to bring to the end
15, 16.		*meḥ*	to fill

17.	*śeṭ*	to gain possession of
21. 22.	*āṭ (ānt)*	part of a fowler's net
23.	*śen*	circuit
25.	*senṭ*	outline for foundation of a building
26.	*ua*	magical knot (?)
27.	*ruṭ*	plant, growing things
28. 29.	*sa*	amulet, protection
30.	*ḥ*	rope
31.	*ḥer*	ḥ + r
32.	*ḥā*	ḥ + ā
34. 35.	*sek*	. . . .
37.	*uaḥ*	to place, be permanent
39.	*uṭen*	offerings
40.	*ṭeben*	to go round about

41.	▱	*rer, peχer,* *ṭeben* }	to go round about
43.	▱	θ (*th*)	. . . .
44.	▱	θ*et* (?)	to take possession of
45.	◯	*ut*	to bandage, substance which has a strong smell
46.	◯	*set*	flowing liquid

22. Vessels.

1. 2.	}	*Bast*	name of a city and of a goddess
4.		*ḥes*	to sing, to praise, to be favoured
5.		*qebḥ*	cold water, coolness
6.		*ḥen*	king, majesty, servant
7.		*neter ḥen*	divine servant, priest
8. 9.	}	*Χent*	what is in front
11.		*χnem*	to unite, to be joined to
14.		*årt*	milk
17.		*teχ*	unguent

20.		*årp*	wine
21.		*nu, qeṭ, neṭ*	liquid
22.		*ån*	to bring
23.		*åb*	heart
25. 26, 27.		*åb, ååb*	to be clean, ceremonially pure
29.		*må*	as, like
31.		*ḥent, åb, useχ*	mistress, lady, broad
33.		*ta*	cake, bread
37, 38.		*χet*	fire
39.		*ba*	bowl containing grains of incense on fire
40.		*ter*	bowl containing fruit (?)
41.		*ḳ*	libation vase
43.		*neb*	lord, all, bowl
44.		*ḳ*	flat bowl with ring handle
49. 50.		*ḥeb*	festival

53.   } *át, beti*   grain, barley and the like
55.

23. Offerings.

1, 2.
3, 4.   } *ta*   bread, cake
5, 6.

10.   *paut*   bread, cake

       paut   company of nine gods

14.   *sep*   time, season

17.   *χ*   a sieve

22.   *ṭā*   to give

23.   *ter*   . . . .

24.   *χemt*   bronze

       ta   . . . .

24. Musical instruments, writing materials, etc.

1.   *ān, sesh*   writing reed, inkpot and pa-lette, to write, to paint

2.   *ṣāt* (?)   a papyrus roll, book

3.		mesen	. . . .
5.		ḥes	to play music
6.		seśeś	sistrum
8.			
9.		nefer	instrument like a lute, **good**
10.		Nefer-Temu	the god Nefer-Temu
11.		sa	syrinx, to know
12.		men	to abide

25. LINE CHARACTERS, ETC.

1.	I	uā	one
2, 4.	||| , ┆ —		sign of plural
5.	\\\	ui	sign of dual
7.	×	seś	to split
9.	∩	met	ten, ∩∩ = taut twenty, ∩∩∩ = māb thirty
10.	⚏, ⚏	ḥerit	fear, awe
11.	⊃	ten	to split, to separate
12.	◠	t	cake

14.	⊢⊣	*teṭ*	what is said
		ki teṭ	"another reading", *i. e.*, variant reading
15.	⊢⊣⊣	*qen, set, āt*	boundary, border
19.	⊂⊃	*ren*	name
20.	⊂⊃	*sen*	to depart
22.	⊿	*seqer*	captive
25.	⌐	*àpt*	part of a palace or temple
27.	⊫	*per, àt, beti*	grain, wheat, barley
29, 30.	∫, ∫	*nem*	. . . .
38, 40.	▦, ▢	*p*	door
46.	⊂⊃	*ḳes*	side, half

CHAPTER V.

PRONOUNS AND PRONOMINAL SUFFIXES.

The personal pronominal suffixes are :—

Sing. 1.	𓇋, 𓀀, 𓀁, 𓀂, 𓏤	Á
„ 2. m.	𓎡	K
„ 2. f.	𓏏, �, 𓀁	T, TH (θ)
„ 3. m.	𓆑	F
„ 3. f.	𓋴 or 𓏤	S
Plur. 1.	𓈖𓏪	N
„ 2.	𓈖𓏪, 𓈖𓏪	TEN, θEN
„ 3.	𓈖𓏪, 𓏤𓈖	SEN

The following examples illustrate their use :—

𓅡𓀀	*ba-à*	my soul
𓊪𓏤𓎡	*seχet-k*	thy field

	emmā-t	with thee
	šuit-f	his shade
	meṭet-s	her words
	à ṭeṭ en-n	what was said by us
	nut-ten	your cities
	ḥāti-sen	their heart.

These suffixes, in the singular, when following a word indicating the noun in the dual, have the dual ending ⸗ *i* added to them; thus ⸗ *merti-fi* "his two eyes"; ⸗ *muti-fi* "his two serpent mothers"; ⸗ *āui-fi* "his two arms"; ⸗ *reṭui-fi* "his two legs".

The forms of the pronouns are :—

I.	Sing. 1.		UÁ
	„ 2. m.		TU, ΘU
	„ 3. m.		SU
	„ 3. f.		SET
	Plur. 1.		N
	„ 2.		TEN, ΘEN
	„ 3.		SEN

II Sing. 1. ⟨hieroglyphs⟩ NUK, ÁNUK

„   2. m. ⟨hieroglyphs⟩ ENTEK, ENTUK

„   2. f. ⟨hieroglyphs⟩ ENTET, ENTUT

„   3. m. ⟨hieroglyphs⟩ ENTEF, ENTUF

„   3. f. ⟨hieroglyphs⟩ ENTES, ENTUS.

Plur. 1. (wanting)

„   2. ⟨hieroglyphs⟩ ENTETEN, ENTUTEN

„   3. ⟨hieroglyphs⟩ ENTESEN, ENTUSEN.

The following are examples of the use of some of these :—

1. ⟨hieroglyphs⟩

ánuk	*paik*	*sen*	*šeráu*
I	thy	brother	younger.

2. ⟨hieroglyphs⟩

ás	*ben*	*ánuk*	*taik*	*muθ*
Behold, not [am] I			thy	mother?

3. ⟨hieroglyphs⟩

entek	*smen*	*ḥer*	*áuset*	*en*	*átef*
Thou [art] stablished upon the seat of the divine father.					

4.   *entef*   *sešem* - *vá*
     He   leadeth   me.

5.   *teṭ*   *en*   *sen*   *án*   *ḥen-f*   *entuten*   *áχ*
     Said   to   them   his majesty,   ye [are]   what?

The **demonstrative pronouns** are :—

Sing. m.		PEN	this
„ f.		TEN	this
„ m.		PEF, PEFA	that
„ f.		TEF, TEFA	that
„ m.		PA	this
„ f.		TA	this.
Plur. m.		ÁPEN, PEN	these
„ f.		ÁPTEN, PETEN	these
„		NEFA	those
„		NA	these
„		PAU	these.

The following are examples of the use of these :—

1. ḥenā ȧp pen

With messenger this.

2. ḥes - sen em ḥetu nu sȧt (?) ten

They shall recite the chapters of book this.

3. ȧs ser pef en Sa sper er

Behold, prince that of Sais went forth to

Ȧneb-ḥetet em uχa

Memphis in the night.

4. ȧs pefa pu teṭ en setem

Behold, that which is said to the listener[s].

5. nuk tefa ḥeṭeṭ sat Rā

I [am] that scorpion the daughter of Rā.

6.   *àmmā - tu*   *àmu-à*   *en*   *ta*

    Grant thou that I may eat   the

   maāst   *en*   *pai*   *àḥ*

    liver   of   this   ox.

7.   *erṭā - nà*   *ḥekau*   *àpen*

    May be given   to me words of power these.

8.   *àn*   *āq*   *qemtu*   *- k*   *em*

    Not shall enter   thy disasters   into

   àt - à   *àpten*

    my members these.

9.   *āḥā - θà erek mà*   *nefa*   *Àsàrtiu*

    Thou art standing like   these   divine Osiris
                                       beings.

10.   *na*   *pu*   *enti*   *em-sa*   *pa*   *χepeš*

    These are   who [are] behind   the   Thigh.

11.

    pau   *setem*   *en* *neteru*

  .....these   heard of the gods.

Other words for "this" are *ennu*, and ⥘⥘,
⥘⥘, or ⥘⥘ *enen*, and they are used thus :—

1.

    ennu   *ennui*   *en* *pet*

  This   canal   of heaven.

2. ⬭⬭ ⬭   ⥘⥘

  ṭā - k   *maa-à*   *enen*   *χeper*

Grant thou [that] I may see this [which] happeneth

  em   *maat - k*

  in   thine eye.

The **relative pronouns** are ⥙𓀁 *à* and *ent*, or
⥙ *enti* or *entet*, and they are used thus :—

1.

    χu   *θenru*   *āśt*   *à*

Glorious things [and] mighty deeds many which

  àri-f   *em*   *suten*

  he did   **as** king.

2.

du	ementuf	à	àri-tu	nef	ḥebsu
It was he		who	made for him		clothes.

3.

ḥest	āat	ent	χer	suten
Favour	great	which [he had]	with	the king.

4.

àrit-nef	àput	neb	enti	em	seχet
He did	errand	every	which [was]	in	the fields.

5.

entet	em	nut - sen
Which [was] in		city their.

The reflexive pronouns are formed by adding the word ⏉𝄐 *tes* to the pronominal suffixes thus :—

		tes-à	myself
		tes-k	thyself
		tes-t	thyself (fem.)
		tes-f	himself
		tes-s	herself
		tes-sen	themselves.

Examples of the use of these are :—

1.

i - nà   *neḍ-à*   *ṭeṭ-à*   *ṭes-à*

I have come, and I have avenged my body my own.

2.

suṭa - kuà   *mà*   *suṭa - k*

I have made myself strong as   thou hast made

tu   *ṭes-k*

strong thyself.

3.

em   *àn*   *neter*   *ṭesef*

In the writing of the god himself.

4.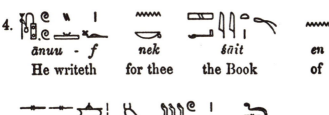

ànuu - f   *nek*   *sàit*   *en*

He writeth   for thee   the Book   of

sensen   *em*   *ṭebàu-f*   *ṭesef*

Breathings   with   his fingers his own.

5.

ṯeṯ	ta	netert	em	re - s	ṯes - s
Speaketh	the goddess	with		her mouth	her own.

6.

χer - sen	her ḥrȧ - sen		em	ta
They fall down	upon face their		in	land

ṯes - sen

heir own.

CHAPTER VI.

NOUNS.

Nouns in Egyptian are either masculine or feminine. Masculine nouns end in U, though this characteristic letter is usually omitted by the scribe, and feminine nouns end in T. Examples of the masculine nouns are :—

𓉐 🐦☉ or 𓉐 🦅☉	*hru*	day
𓇋𓏤🧍	*ānu*	scribe
𓏏𓎛🦅𓎟	*ḳerḥu*	night,

but these words are just as often written 𓉐☉, 𓇋𓏤, and 𓏏𓎛𓎟. Other examples are :—

𓊪𓏤	*ȧp*	envoy
𓎡𓏤𓎗	*qeres*	sepulchre
𓊹	*neter*	god
𓂋𓏤	*re*	chapter, mouth.

Examples of feminine nouns are :—

šāt	book
pet	heaven
seχet	field
sebχet	pylon
netert	goddess
ţept	boat.

Masculine nouns in the plural end in U or IU, and feminine nouns in the plural in UT, but often the T is not written; examples are :—

ānχiu	living beings
āšemu	the forms in which the gods appear
ḥau	people who live in the Delta.
sbau	doors
suteniu netiu (or *bàtiu*)	Kings of the South and North
ḥemut	women
satut	daughters
meḥut	offerings
àsut	places.

The oldest way of expressing the plural is by writing the ideograph or picture sign three times, as the following examples taken from early texts will shew :—

reṭ	legs
χu	spirits
per	houses, habitations
ḥemut	women
nut	cities
seχet	fields
uat	ways, roads.

Sometimes the picture sign is written once with three dots, $\substack{\circ \\ \circ \\ \circ}$ or ○○○, placed after it thus :—

χu	spirits

The three dots or circles $\substack{\circ \\ \circ}$ afterwards became modified into | or ||| , and so became the common sign of the plural.

Words spelt in full with alphabetic or syllabic signs are also followed at times by $\substack{\circ \\ \circ}$:—

reθ	men
ḥunut	young women

	urâu	great ones
	šerru	little ones.

The plural is also expressed in the earliest times by writing the word in alphabetic or syllabic signs followed by the determinative written thrice :—

	ḫāt	hearts
	besek	intestines
	ārrt	abodes
	qesu	bones
	seteb	obstacles
	ermen	arms
	àχemu-seku	a class of stars
	seχet	fields
	seb	stars
	petet	bows
	tām	sceptres.

In the oldest texts the dual is usually expressed by adding UI or TI to the noun, or by doubling the picture sign thus :— 👁 the two eyes, 🦻 🦻 the two ears, ⚊ the two hands, ⚊ the two lips, and the like. Frequently the word is spelt alphabetically or syllabically and is determined by the double picture sign, thus :—

	the two divine souls
	the double heaven, *i. e.*, North and South
	the two sides
	the two lights.

Instead of the repetition of the picture sign two strokes, ‖ were added to express the dual, thus Ḥāp, the double Nile-god. But in later times the two strokes were confused with ⑊, which has the value of I, and the word is also written ; but in each case the reading is *Ḥāpui*. The following are examples of the use of the dual :—

1.

årit - nef teχenui urui em mat

He made two obelisks great of granite

2.

pa　　*teχenui*　　　*urui*

The　　two obelisks　　great.

3.

nefer   *ḥrà*   *em*   *śuti*   *urui*

Beautiful of face with two plumes great.

4.

er   *àmtu*   *beχenti*   *urti*

Between   the two pylons great.

5.

Baui-fi   *pui*   *en*   *àmu*   *Ṭeṭet*

His double soul   that   which [is] in   Tattu (Busiris).

6.

baui   *ḥer-àb*   *tafui*

The divine souls within the two divine Tchafui.

7.

baui-fi   *ḥer-àbui*   *tafui*   *ba*

His double soul within the two Tchafui [are] the soul

pu   *en*   *Rā*   *ba*   *pu*   *en*   *Àsàr*

of   Rā, [and] the soul   of   Osiris.

8.

χā - kuà   *em*   *sati - θen*

I have risen   as   two daughters your.

9. [hieroglyphs]

ảnet ḥràu - θen Reḥti Senti

Homage to you [ye] two opponents, [ye] two sisters,

[hieroglyphs]

Merti

[ye] two Mert goddesses.

10. [hieroglyphs]

ṭep àui senti - k.

Upon the two hands of thy two sisters.

———

CHAPTER VII.

THE ARTICLE.

The **definite article** masculine is 𓅮 or 𓅮𓅮 PA, the feminine is 𓏏𓅮 TA, and the plural is 𓅮 NA or 𓅮 NA EN; the following examples will explain the use of the article.

1.

𓅮	𓊪	𓎡	𓅓	𓅮𓅮	𓈙
na	pu	enti	em-sa	pa	χepeś
Those are	who [are]		behind	the	star Thigh

𓅓	𓊪
em	pet
in	heaven.

2.

𓅮𓅮	𓊲	𓈖	𓊨	�	𓅮𓅮
pa	bes	en	seśet	ḥnā	pa
The flame		of	fire	and	the

𓎁	𓈖	𓏏
uat	en	θeḥent
tablet	of	crystal.

3.

nuk	*pa*	*ba*	*en*	*ta*	*χat*	*āāt*
I [am]	the	Soul	of	the	Body	great.

4.

reχ - *kuȧ*	*ren*	*en*	*pa*	*neter*
I know	the name	of	the	god[s]

XLII	*en*	*uneniu*	*henā* - *k*
forty-two	who	exist	with thee.

5.

nefer	*pa*	*stimu*	*em*	*ta*	*ȧset*
Good [is]	the	grass	in	the	place

ment
such and such.

6.

ta	*hemt*	*en*	*paif*	*sen*	*āa*
The	wife	of	his	brother	elder

ȧu - *tu*	*hems*	*her*	*nebṭ* - *set*
she	was sitting	at	her hair.[1]

[1] *I. e.,* she was sitting dressing her hair.

7. na — *šeršeru* — en — *p[a]* — *ášeṭ*
    The — winds (air) — of — the — acacia tree

    šeps — en — *Ánnu*
    venerable — of — Ánnu.

8. *áu-f* — *her* — *χaṭbu* — *taif* — *ḥemt*
    He — slew — his — wife,

    áu-f — *her* — *χaā - set* — *na* — *en* — *áu*
    he — threw her [to] — the — dogs.

9. *un* — *án* — *pa* — *sti* — . . . . — *her* — *χeperu* — *em*
    The — smell — became — in

    na — *en* — *ḥebsu* — *en* — *Áa-perti*
    the — garments — of — Pharaoh.

The masculine indefinite article is expressed by *uā en*, and the feminine by *uāt en*; the words *uā en* and *uāt en* mean, literally, "one of". Examples are :—

1. [hieroglyphs]

qeṭ - nef	uā	en	beⲭennu	em
He built	a house			with

[hieroglyphs]

ṭet - f	em	ta	ȧnt	pa	āś
his own hand in	the	valley	of	the cedar.	

2. [hieroglyphs]

ȧu-f	ḥer	ȧn	uā	en	sfenṭ	ḳesȧ
He		brought			a knife [for cutting] reeds.	

3. [hieroglyphs]

ȧⲭ	qeṭ - k	uā	en	set	ḥemt
O	fashion thou	a		wife	

[hieroglyphs]

en	Batau
for	Batau.

4. [hieroglyphs]

ⲭer	ȧr	ȧu-k	qem - f	emtuk
When	thou		findest it,	thou shalt

ḥer   ṭātu-f   er   uā   en   ḳai   en

put   it   into   a   pot   of

mu   qebḥ   ka   ānχ - ȧ

water   cold, [and] verily   I shall live.

5. ȧu   pa   Rā   ḥer   ṭāt   χeperu   uā   en

   The Rā   caused   to become   a

mu   āa   er   duṭ - f   er   duṭ

stream great   between   him [and]   between

paif   sen   āȧ

his   brother elder.

From the union of the definite article with the personal suffixes is formed the following series of words:—

MASCULINE.   FEMININE.

pai-ȧ   tai-ȧ

𓅃𓏭𓏮 *pai-k*		𓅊𓏭𓏮 *tai-k*	
𓅃𓏭𓁐 *pai-t*		𓅊𓏭 *tai-t*	
𓅃𓏭			
𓅃𓏭 *pai-f*		𓅊𓏭 *tai-f*	
𓅃𓏭 *pai-s*	}	𓅊𓏭 *tai-s*	}
𓅃𓏭 *pai-set*		𓅊𓏭 *tai-set*	
𓅃𓏭 *pai-n*		𓅊𓏭 *tai-n*	
𓅃𓏭 *pai-ten*		𓅊𓏭 *tai-ten*	
𓅃𓏭 *pai-sen*		𓅊𓏭 *tai-sen*	
𓅃𓏭 *pai-u*		𓅊𓏭 *tai-u*	

COMMON.

𓅓𓏭 *nai-á*		𓅓𓏭 *nai-n*	
𓅓𓏭 *nai-á*			
𓅓𓏭 *nai-k*		𓅓𓏭 *nai-ten*	
𓅓𓏭 *nai-0*	}		
𓅓𓏭 *nai-t*			
𓅓𓏭 *nai-f*		𓅓𓏭 *nai-sen*	
𓅓𓏭 *nai-s*		𓅓𓏭 *nai-u*	

The following examples will illustrate their use :—

1.

pai-à	*sen*	*āa*	*ḥer*	*sànnu* - *nà*
My	brother	elder		hurried me.

2.

pai-à	*neb*	*nefer*
My	lord	beautiful.

3.

àχ	*pai - k*	*i*	*em - sa-à*	*er*
Fie on	thy	coming	after me	to

χaṭbu
slay [me].

4.

χer	*pai-t*	*hai*	*emmā-à*
For	thy	husband [is]	to me

em	*seχeru*	*en*	*àtef*
in	the guise	of	a father.

5. *ȧs* *ta* *ḥemt* *en* *pai-f* *sen* *āa*
   Behold the wife of his brother elder

senṭu - Oȧ
was afraid.

6. *ȧu - set* *ḥer* *ṭeṭ* *en* *pai - set* *sȧu*
   She said to her keeper.

7. *ȧu* *ḥāti - sen* *ḥer* *neṭem* *ḥer* *pai - sen*
   Were their hearts rejoicing over their

rā *baku*
doing of work.

8. *temit* *uχaā* *tai-ȧ* *māȧu·*
   That not may fall my hair

ḥer *uat*
on the way

9.

tai-k	*šāi*	*āš-θȧ em*	*nasaqu*
Thy	letter	abounds in	**breaks.**

10.

suten	*neb*	*ḥenā*	*tai-u*	*suten*	*ḥemut*
King[s]	all	with	their		queens.

1.

ȧmmā	*ȧn - tu - nȧ*	*nai-ȧ*	*uru*
Let be	brought to me	my	nobles

āaiu
great.

2.

er	*nai-k*	*re-ḥet*	*āaiu*
To	thy	storehouses	great

em   Uast
in Thebes.

3.

nai-f	*en*	*χarṭu*
His		children.

4.

χer	nai - sen		χāi	en	rā	āš-
With	their		weapons,			numerous

set	em	śā

were they as the sand.

5.

nai-u	qerāu	em	χemt
Their	bolts	of	copper (or bronze).

6.

keteχ	em	ḥerti	ḥer	naiu	āā
Goods	on	porter[s]	and upon	their	asses.

7.

ṭāu-ȧ	ḥems		reχit		em
I caused to sit			the people		in

nai-u	qubu	ṭāu-ȧ	śemi	ta
their	shadow.	I caused	to travel	the

set	Ta-merȧ	itu - s	seuseχ-θ
woman	of Egypt	on her journey	making long [her
			journey]

er	àset	mer - nes	àn	teha-
to	the place	she wished [to go],	not	attacked

set	kaui	bu-nebu	her	uat
her	any person	whatsoever	on the way

ADJECTIVES, NUMERALS, TIME, THE YEAR, ETC.

The **adjective** is, in form, often similar to the noun, with which it agrees in gender and number ; with a few exceptions it comes after its noun, thus :—

xet   nebt   nefert   ābt   xet   nebt   netemet beneret

Thing every, good, pure; thing every, pleasant, sweet.

The following will explain the use of the adjective in the singular and plural.

1.

ānx-ȧ   em   tau   en   beti   hetet

Let me live upon   bread   of   barley   white,

heqet-ȧ   em   pertu   teseru

my ale [made] of   grain   red.

2.

àu	*ḥen*	*ḥer*	*ḥems*	*ḥer*	*àrit*	*ḥru*
Was	[His] Majesty	sitting		to	make	a day

nefer	*er*	*ḥenā - set*
happy		with her.

3.

qem - k	*ta*		*šerāu*	*nefer*
Thou didst find	the		girl	pretty

ta	*enti*	*ḥer*	*sau*	*na*	*kamu*
who	was	watching	the		gardens.

4.

ka	*àri-à*	*nek*	*ḥebsu*	*neferu*
Indeed	I will make	for thee	clothes	beautiful.

5.

àu - sen	*ḥer*	*ruṭ*	*em*	*šauabu*
They	grew		into	trees

sen	*āaiu*
two	great.

6. [hieroglyphs]

àu-à   *em - baḥ*   *neteru*   *āaiu*

I am in the presence of the gods   great.

The adjectives "royal" and "divine" are usually written before the noun, thus :—

[hieroglyphs]	*suten ān*	royal scribe
[hieroglyphs]	*suten ḥemu*	royal workman
[hieroglyphs]	*suten uaà*	royal boat *or* barge
[hieroglyphs]	*suten reχ*	royal acquaintance *or* kinsman
[hieroglyphs]	*suten ḥemt*	royal woman, *i. e.,* queen
[hieroglyphs]	*sutenu ḥenu*	royal servants
[hieroglyphs]	*neter ḥen*	divine servant, *i. e.,* priest
[hieroglyphs]	*neter ḥet*	divine house, *i. e.,* temple
[hieroglyphs]	*neter àtef*	divine father.

Adjectives are without degrees of comparison in Egyptian, but the comparative and superlative may be expressed in the following manner :—

1.

āu - set   *nefer*   *em*   *ḫāt - set*   *er*   *set*

She was   fair   in   her body   more than

ḥemt   *nebt*   *enti*   *em*   *pa*   *ta*   *ter - f*

woman   any   who [was] in   the   earth the whole of it.

2.

ur - k   *er*   *neteru*

Great art thou more than   the gods.

3.

se - āśt - u   *er*   *śā*

They were numerous more than the sand.

4.

āneḏ   *ḥrā - k*   *χu*   *er*   *neteru*

Homage to thee [O thou one] glorious more than the gods.

5.

betenu   *er*   *θesemu*   *χaχet*

Fleet   more than   greyhounds,   swift

er   *śuit*

more than   light.

6. χeper   àqer - k   eref   em

It shall happen   thou shalt be wise   more than   he by

ķer

being silent.

7. nefer   setem   er   entet   neb

Good is hearkening more than anything, *i. e.,* to obey
is best of all.

NUMERALS.

I	=		uä	= 1
II	=		sen	= 2
III	=		χcmet	= 3
IIII	=	or	fţu or àfţu	= 4
II III ★	=		ţuau	= 5
III III	=		sàs	= 6
III IIII	=		sefeχ	= 7

‖‖ ‖‖	=	(hieroglyphs)	χemennu	= 8
‖‖ ‖‖‖	=	(hieroglyphs)	pest	= 9
∩	=	(hieroglyphs)	met	= 10
∩∩	=	(hieroglyphs)	taut	= 20
∩∩∩	=	(hieroglyphs)	māb	= 30
∩∩ ∩∩	=	(hieroglyphs)	ḥement	= 40
∩∩ ∩∩∩	=	(?)	(?)	= 50
∩∩∩ ∩∩∩	=	(?)	(?)	= 60
∩∩∩ ∩∩∩∩	=	(hieroglyphs)	sefeχ	= 70
∩∩∩∩ ∩∩∩∩	=	(hieroglyphs)	χemennui	= 80
∩∩∩∩ ∩∩∩∩∩	=	(?)	(?)	= 90
℮	=	(hieroglyphs)	śaā	= 100
(hieroglyph)	=	(hieroglyphs)	χa	= 1000
⎮	=	(hieroglyphs)	tāb	= 10,000
(frog)	=	(hieroglyphs)	ḥefennu	= 100,000

𓁨	=	𓁨𓁨𓁨	*ḥeḥ* = 1,000,000
𓈗	=		*šennu* = 10,000,000

The ordinals are formed by adding ○ *nu* to the numeral, with the exception of "first", thus :—

	Masc.		Fem.	
First	𓁐	*ţepi*	𓁐	*ţept*
Second	II ○		II ○	
Third	III ○		III ○	
Fourth	IIII ○		IIII ○	
Fifth	IIIII ○		IIIII ○	
Sixth	III III ○		III III ○	
Seventh	III IIII ○		III IIII ○	
Eighth	IIII IIII ○		IIII IIII ○	
Ninth	IIII IIIII ○		IIII IIIII ○	
Tenth	∩ ○		∩ ○	

and so on. From the following examples of the use of the numerals it will be noticed that the numeral, like the adjective, is placed *after* the noun, that the lesser numeral comes last, and that the noun is sometimes in the singular and sometimes in the plural.

1.

rex - kuȧ   ren   en   pa   neter   XLII

    I know   the name of   the   god forty-two,

i. e., I know the names of the forty-two gods.

2.

re   en   tekau   IV

Chapter of   the flames   four, *i. e.,* "four flames".

3.

nes   su   xet   300   em   au-f

Belong   to him measure[s] 300   in   his length,

xet   230   em   usext-f

measure[s]   230   in   his breadth.

4.

meḥ   1000   pu   em   au-f

Cubit[s] one thousand is he in   his length.

5.

ṯāu-ȧ   nek   met   en   ṯebā   en   ṯep   en

I have given to thee { 10   of 10,000 } of bushels of
                            i. e., tens of ten
                              thousands

neferu   er   setefau   neter-ḥetep-k

grain   for   the supply   of thy offerings.

6.

âqu   *âaiu* $(100{,}000 \times 9) + (10{,}000 \times 9)$

Loaves large,   900,000   +   90,000

$+ (1000 \times 2) + (100 \times 7) + (10 \times 5)$

$+ \quad 2000 \quad + \quad 700 \quad + \quad 50$

i. e., 992,750 large loaves of bread.

7. In the papyrus of Rameses III we have the following numbers of various kinds of geese set out and added up thus :—

			==	6820
			=	1410
			=	1534
			=	150
			=	4060
			=	25020
			=	57810
			=	21700
			=	1240
			=	6510

Total $(10{,}000 \times 9) + (1000 \times 32) + (100 \times 40) + (10 \times 25) + 4 = 126{,}254$

Ordinal numbers are also indicated by ⌒ *meḥ,* which is placed before the figure thus :—

1.

em	*maāu*	*meḥ*	*uā*	*em*	*maāu*

In　the temples of the first [rank], in　the temples

meḥ	*sen*

of the second [rank].

TIME.

The principal divisions of time are :—

ḥat	second		*at*	minute
unnut	hour		*hru*	day
ābeṭ	month		*renpit*	year
seṭ	30 years		*ḥen*	60 years
ḥenti	120 years		*ḥeḥ*	100,000 years
ḥeḥ	1,000,000 years		*tetta*	eternity.

sen 10,000,000

Examples of the use of these are :—

1.

ṭā - f	*renput*	*āšt*		*her*	*her*	*renput-ā*
May he give	years	many		over and	above	my years

ent | ānχ | àbeṭu | āś | ḥer
of | life; [and] months | | many | { over, *i. e.*, } { in addition to }

àbet-à | nu | ānχ | hru | āś | ḥer
my months | of | life; [and] days | | many over

hru-à | nu | ānχ | ḳerḥ | āś | ḥer
my days of | life; [and] nights | | many | over

ḳerḥ - à
my nights.

2.
untet - f | ḥenti | ḥeḥ
His existence is [for] 120 years × 100,000 years.

3.
uneniu | ānχ | er | neḥeḥ | ḥenti
Who exist | living | for | ever, | 120 years ×

ṭetta
eternity.

4. 〔hieroglyphs〕

au - k   er   ḥeḥ   en   ḥeḥ

Thou art   for millions of years of millions of years,

〔hieroglyphs〕

āḥā   ḥeḥ

a period of millions of years.

This was the answer which the god Thoth made to the scribe Ani when he asked him how long he had to live, and was written about the XVIth century B.C. The same god told one of the Ptolemies that he had ordained the sovereignty of the royal house for a period of time equal to :—

〔hieroglyphs〕

tetta   ḥenti   ḥeḥ   seṭu

An eternity of 120 year periods, an infinity of 30 year periods,

〔hieroglyphs〕

ḥeḥ   renput   šenu ābeṭ   ḥefnu

millions of years, ten millions of months, hundreds of thousands

〔hieroglyphs〕

hru   ṭebāu   unnut   χau   at

of days, tens of thousands of hours, thousands of minutes,

šaā	*ḥat*	*met*	*ȧnt*

hundreds of seconds, [and] tens of thirds of **seconds**

The Egyptian Year.

The year, 〰〰 *renpit*, plural 〰〰 consisted originally of twelve months, each containing thirty days ; as the month contained three periods of ten days the year consisted of thirty-six weeks of ten days each. Later the Egyptians added five days[1] to the years, and thus made it equal to 365 days ℮℮℮ 〰〰.[2] Each month was dedicated to a god. The twelve months were divided into three seasons of four months each, thus :—

1. *akhet* season of inundation and period of sowing.

2. *pert* season of "coming forth" or growing, *i.e.*, spring.

3. *šemut* season of harvest and beginning of inundation.

Documents were dated thus :—

[1] Called "epagomenal days".

[2] They discovered that the true year was longer than 365 days, that the difference between 365 days and the length of the true year was equal nearly to one day in four years, and that New Year's day ran through the whole year in $365 \times 4 = 1460$ years.

1.   *renpit IV*   *àbeṭ IV*   *akhet*   *hru 1*

Year four, month four of the sowing season, day one

χer   *ḥen*   *en*

under the majesty of, etc.

i. e., the first day of the fourth month of the sowing season in the fourth year of the reign of king So-and-so.

2.   *renpit V*   *àbeṭ III*   *šemut*   *hru peṣṭ χer*

Year five, month three of inundation, day nine under

ḥen   *en suten net* (or *bàt*) *Usr-Maāt-Rā-setep-en-Rā*

the majesty of { the king of the South and North } Usr-Maāt-Rā-setep-en-Rā,

sa Rā   *Rā-meses-meri-Ámen*

son of the Sun, Rameses, beloved of Amen, etc.

3.   *renpit XXI*   *àbeṭ I*   *akhet*   *χer*

Year twenty-one, month one of sowing season under

ḥen	en	suten bȧt	Ȧmen meri Piȧnχi

the majesty of { the king of the South and North, } Piȧnkhi beloved of Amen.

4. renpit IX   Apalius   sesu   VII

Year nine   of Apellaeus,   day   seven,

ṭep   per   hru   XVII   en   ȧmu

first[month] of spring, day seventeen of the dwellers in

Ta-mert   χer   ḥen   suten bȧt

{ Ta-mert, i. e., Egypt } under the majesty of { the king of the South and North }

Ptualmis   ȧnχ   tetta   Ptaḥ meri

Ptolemy, living for ever, beloved of Ptah.

This date shews that there was a difference of ten days between the dating in use among the priests and that of the Egyptians in the time of Ptolemy III Euergetes, king of Egypt from B. C. 247 to B. C. 222.

4. renpit XXXII   ȧbeṭ   III   šemut   hru   VI

Year thirty-two, month three of sowing season, day six

χer	*ḥen*	*suten bāt*
under	the divine majesty of	{ the king of the South and North, }

Rā-usr-maāt - meri - Āmen	*ānχ*	*uţa*
Rā-usr-maāt - meri - Amen,	life!	strength!

senb	*sa Rā*	*Rāmeses*	*ḥeq Ānnu*
health!	son of the Sun,	Rameses,	prince of Heliopolis.

The words ☥ ⎮ ∩, which frequently follow royal names, may be also translated "Life to him! Strength to him! Health to him!" They often occur after any mention of or reference to the king, thus :—

1. *pa*	*θáireåa*	*āa*	*en*	*Āa-perti*
The	door	great	of	Pharaoh,

ānχ	*uţa*	*senb*
life!	strength!	health!

2.

uā	*en*	*suten*	*ḥemu*	*ṭep*	*en*	*ḥen - f*
One		royal	workman	first	of	His Majesty,

ānχ   *uṭa*   *senb*

life! strength! health!

It has been said above that each month was dedicated to a god, and it must be noted that the month was called after the god's name. The Copts or Egyptian Christians have preserved, in a corrupt form, the old Egyptian names of the months, which they arrange in the following order :—

1st month of winter = Thoth

2nd „   „ = Paopi

3rd „   „ = Hathor

4th „   „ = Khoiak

1st month of spring = Tobi

2nd „   „ = Mekhir

3rd „   „ = Phamenoth

4th „   „ = Pharmuthi

𓏤		1st month of summer	=		Pakhon
𓏥	„	2nd „ „	=		Paoni
𓏦	„	3rd „ „	=		Epep
𓏤𓏤𓏤𓏤	„	4th „ „	=		Mesore.

The epagomenal days were called ⊙ ||||| ⌐ ℮ ||| { ⌐
"the five days over (*i. e.*, to be added to) the year".

CHAPTER IX.

THE VERB.

The consideration of the Egyptian verb, or stem-word, is a difficult subject, and one which can only be properly illustrated by a large number of extracts from texts of all periods. Egyptologists have, moreover, agreed neither as to the manner in which it should be treated, nor as to the classification of the forms which have been distinguished. The older generation of scholars were undecided as to the class of languages under which the Egyptian language should be placed, and contented themselves with pointing out grammatical forms analogous to those in Coptic, and perhaps in some of the Semitic dialects; but recently the relationship of Egyptian to the Semitic languages has been boldly affirmed, and as a result the nomenclature of the Semitic verb or stem-word has been applied to that of Egyptian.

The Egyptian stem-word may be indifferently a verb or a noun; thus 🪲 *χeper* means "to be, to become", and the "thing which has come into being". By the addition of ⌫ 𓀀 the stem-word obtains a participial meaning like "being" or "becoming"; by the addition of 𓃀 ||| in the masc. and ⌒)||| in the fem. χeper becomes a noun in the plural meaning "things which exist", "created things", and the like; and by the addition of ⟨𓏭 we have 𓆣⟨𓏭 χeperȧ the god to whom the property of creating men and things belonged. The following examples will illustrate the various uses of the word :—

1.

neter   *uȧu*   *χeper*   *em*   *sep*   *ṭep*

The god one [who] came into being in time primeval.

2.

χeper   *meṭet*   *nebt*   *Tem*

Came into being   words   all   of Tem.

3.

ȧn   *χepert*   *sat*   *ṭu*

Not had come into being earth [and] mountains.

4.

saut   *χepert*   *θui*   *ȧat*

Guarding   { thing that hath {   that   great.
          { come into being }

5.

àri-à   χeperu   neb   er   ṭāṭā

I have made   transformations   all   at the dictates

àb-à   em   bu   neb   mer   ka-à

of my heart in   place every [which] wished my *ka*.

6.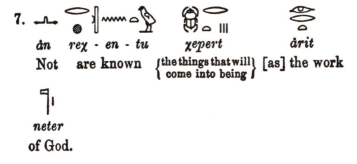

em   ḥrà   en   χeperu   ḥā   i - ḥer - sa

In the face of men and women and those who shall come

sen

after them.

7.

àn   reχ - en - tu   χepert   àrit

Not   are known   {the things that will come into being}   [as] the work

neter

of God.

8.

χeper-à   χeper   χeperu

{I am he who came into being} and {who made to come into being} {the beings who came into being} χeperu   -   kuȧ   em   χeperu   en

I came   into being   in   the forms   of

χeperȧ   χeper   em   sep   ṭepi

the god Khepera, who came into being in primeval time.

Or again, if we take a word like ȧqer it will be seen from the following examples that according to its position and use in a sentence it becomes a noun, or a verb, or an adjective, or an adverb.

1.   sma-ȧ   em   χu   śepsi   ȧqer

    May I join   the spirits   holy [and] perfect

nu   neter-χert

of the underworld.

2.   śȧt (?)   ent   sȧqer   χu

    The book   of   making { perfect or strong } { the spirit [of the] deceased]. }

3.   ȧu-f   netri   emmā   ȧqeru

    He is   divine   among   the perfect ones.

4. $\dot{a}u$ - sen $\dot{a}aut$ $enti$ er - $\dot{h}\bar{a}ti$-f

They,   the cattle which were   before   him

$\dot{h}er$ $\chi eperu$ $nefer$ er $\dot{a}qer$ sep sen

became   fine,   exceedingly, twice.

I. e., the cattle became very fine indeed.

Stem-words in Egyptian, like those in Hebrew and other Semitic dialects, consist of two, three, four, and five letters, which are usually consonants, one or more of which may be vowels, as examples of which may be cited :—

	$\bar{a}n$	to return, go or send back
	ha	to walk
	$\bar{a}\dot{h}a$	to stand
	$\dot{s}\bar{a}t$	to cut
	$rerem$	to weep
	$ne\dot{k}a$	to cut
	$nemmes$	to enlighten
	$net net$	to converse

	nemesmes	to heap up to over-flowing.
	netemnetem	(probably pronounced *netemtem*) to love.

The stem-words with three letters or consonants, which are ordinarily regarded as triliteral roots, may be reduced to two consonants, which were pronounced by the help of some vowel between; these we may call primary or biliteral roots. Originally all roots consisted of one syllable. By the addition of feeble consonants in the middle or at the end of the monosyllabic root, or by repeating the second consonant, roots of three letters were formed. Roots of four consonants are formed by adding a fourth consonant, or by combining two roots of two letters; and roots of five consonants from two triliteral roots by the omission of one consonant.

Speaking generally, the Egyptian verb has no conjugation or species like Hebrew and the other Semitic dialects, and no Perfect (Preterite) or Imperfect (Future) tenses. The exact pronunciation of a great many verbs must always remain unknown, because the Egyptians never invented a system of vocalisation, and never took the trouble to indicate the various vowel sounds like the Syrians and Arabs; but by comparing forms which are common both to Egyptian and Coptic, a tolerably correct idea of the pronunciation may be obtained.

There is in Egyptian a derivative formation of the

word-stem or verb, which is made by the addition of S, —— or ⌠, to the simple form of the verb, and which has a causative signification; in Coptic the causative is expressed both by a prefixed S and T. The following are examples of the use of the Egyptian causative:—

1. From 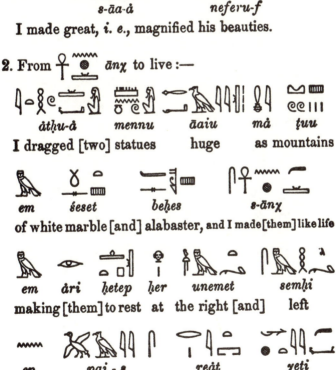 *āa* to be great:—

s-āa-ȧ   *neferu-f*

I made great, *i. e.*, magnified his beauties.

2. From ♀〰️◯ *ānχ* to live:—

ȧtḥu-ȧ	*mennu*	*āaiu*	*mȧ*	*ṭuu*
I dragged [two] statues		huge		as mountains

em	*šeset*	*beḥes*	*s-ānχ*
of white marble [and] alabaster, and I made [them] like life

em	*ȧri*	*ḥetep*	*her*	*unemet*	*semḥi*
making [them] to rest	at	the right [and]			left

en	*pai - s*	*reȧt*	*χeti*
of	its	door	inscribed

ḥer   ren   ur   ḥen - k

with   the name   great of thy majesty.

3. From   χeper to become :—

seχeperu   -   nȧ   re-ḫetu-f

I made to come   into being   his treasure-houses

bāḥ   em   χet   ta   neb

[which were] flooded with things of every land.

The verb with pronominal personal suffixes is as follows :—

Sing.			
1 com.		reχ-ȧ	I know
2 m.		neḥem-k	thou deliverest
2 f.		teṭ-t	thou speakest
3 m.		sāṭ-f	he cuts
3 f.		qem-s	she finds
Plur.			
1 com.		ȧri-n	we do
2 com.		mit-ten	ye die
3 com.		χeper-sen	they become.

The commonest auxiliary verbs are ⟨hieroglyphs⟩ *āḥā* to stand ; ⟨hieroglyphs⟩ *un* to be ; ⟨hieroglyphs⟩ *àu* to be ; ⟨hieroglyphs⟩ *àri* to do ; ⟨hieroglyphs⟩ *ṭā* to give ; the following passages illustrate their use :—

1.

un	*àn - f*	*ḥer*	*teṭ*	*nes*	*set*	*āḥā*
Was he		saying		to her,		'Stand up

ṭā-t	*nà*	*pertu*
give thou to me		grain'.

2.

āḥā	*teṭ - set*	*nef*	*bu*	*pu*	*uā*	*meṭet*
Stood up	said she to him,		'No one			hath spoken

enṭmā-à	*ḥeru*	*paìk*	*sen*	*šeràu*
with me	except	thy	young brother'.

3.

āḥā	*en*	*qemḥet*	*en*	*set*
Stood up		glanced	at	them

ḥen - f	*āḥā - nef*	*χāra*	*er*
His Majesty,	he stood up	furious with rage	against

sen	mā	tef	Menθu	neb	Uast
them	like	father	Menthu,	lord of Thebes.

1.

un	ȧn - s	set	ḥer	aḥā
Was	she		standing up.

2.

un	ȧn - f	ḥer	teṭtu	emmā - s
Was	he		speaking	with her

set	em	teṭ
	saying :—

3.

un	ȧn - f	ḥer	ārqu - f	en
Was	he	taking an oath to him	by

pa	Rā - Ḥeru - χuti	em	teṭ
the god Rā - Harmachis,	saying :—

4.

un	ȧn	pa	āteṭu	en	ḥer
Was		the	young man	coming (?) to

meṭu	*emmā*	*paif*	*sen*
speak	with	his	brother.

1.

àu - à	*senṭ - kuà*	*en*	*baiu-k*
I am	fearing		thy souls (*i. e.*, will).

2.

àu - f	*ḥer*	*sper*	*er*	*paif*	*per*
Was he		going	into	his	house,

àu - f	*ḥer*	*qem*	*taif*	*ḥemt*
was he		finding	his	wife

seṭer - θà	*mer - θà*	*en*	*āṭau*
lying	sick	through	{ violent treatment.}

àu - set	*ḥer*	*temt*	*ṭàt*	*mu*	*ḥer*	*ṭet - f*
Was she		not	putting	water	upon	his hand

em	*paif*	*seχeru*	*àu*	*bu*	*pui*
according	to his	wont.		Was not

set	setau	er - ḥāt - f	au	paif
she	lighting a fire	before him.	Was	his

per	em	kekui
house	in	darkness.

1.

māāi	ari - n	en - n	unnut
Come,	let us make	for ourselves	an hour

seteru
lying down.

2.

em	ari	meḥ	ab - k	aχetu
[Do] not make	to fill	heart thy	[with] the wealth

kai
of another.

1.

ben	au-a	er	ṭāt	per - f	em
Not	am I		letting	to come forth it	from

re - å   en   reθ   nebt
my mouth to   people   any.

2.   emtuf   ån   naif   åaut
     He   brought   his   cattle

er - ḥāt - f   er   ṭāt   sefer - u   em
before him   to   make   lie down them in

pai - sen   åhait
their   stalls.

In the limits of this little book it is impossible to set
before the reader examples of the use of the various
parts of the verb, and to illustrate the forms of it which
have been identified with the Infinitive and Imperative
moods and with participial forms. If the Egyptian verb
is to be treated as a verb in the Semitic languages we
should expect to find forms corresponding to the Kal,
Niphal, Piel, Pual, Hiphil, Shaphel, and other conju-
gations, according as we desired to place it in the
Southern or Northern group of Semitic dialects. Forms
undoubtedly exist which lend themselves readily to
Semitic nomenclature, but until all the texts belonging

to all periods of the Egyptian language have been published, that is to say, until all the material for grammatical investigation has been put into the Egyptologists' hands, it is idle to attempt to make a final set of grammatical rules which will enable the beginner to translate any and every text which may be set before him. In many sentences containing numerous particles only the general sense of the text or inscription will enable him to make a translation which can be understood. In a plain narrative the verb is commonly a simple matter, but the addition of the particles occasions great difficulty in rendering many passages into a modern tongue, and only long acquaintance with texts will enable the reader to be quite certain of the meaning of the writer at all times. Moreover, allusions to events which took place in ancient times, with the traditions of which the writer was well acquainted, increase the difficulty. This being so it has been thought better to give at the end of the sketch of Egyptian grammar a few connected extracts from texts, with interlinear transliteration and translation, so that the reader may judge for himself of the difficulties which attend the rendering of the Egyptian verb into English.

———

CHAPTER X.

ADVERBS, PREPOSITIONS, CONJUNCTIONS, PARTICLES.

ADVERBS.

In Egyptian the prepositions and certain substantives and adjectives to which ⬭ *er* is prefixed take the place of adverbs; examples are :—

1. The cattle which were before him became

nefer	*er*	*àqer*	*sep sen*	*qeb - sen*
fine	exceedingly,	twice,	they doubled

mesu - sen	*er*	*àqer sep sen*
their births	exceedingly, twice.

2.

un	*set*	*nefer*	*er*	*āa - ur*	*ḥer àb*
Was the woman fair	exceedingly	to the mind

en   ḥen-f   er   χet   neb

of his majesty more than any thing.

3. au - f   senṭ   er   āa - ur

    Was he   afraid   exceedingly.

4. χāqu - tu   pa   ḥetrā   er

    Were cut (wounded) the   horses

ennuit

immediately.

PREPOSITIONS.

Prepositions, which may also be used adverbially,
are simple and compound. The simple prepositions
are :—

1. ∿ *en*   for, to, in, because.

2. 𓅿 *em*   from, out of, in, into, on, among, as,
                conformably to, with, in the state of,
                if, when.

3. ⬯ *er*   to, into, against, by, at, from, until.

4. 𓁶 or 𓁶 *ḥer* upon, besides, for, at, on account of.

5. 𓁶 *ṭep*   upon.

6. χer   under, with.

7. χer   from, under, with, during.

8. mā   from, by.

9. henā   with.

10. χeft   in the face of, before, at the time of.

11. χent   in front of, at the head of.

12. ḥa   behind.

13. mȧ   like, as.

14. ter   since, when, as soon as.

The following are used as prepositions:—

ȧmi   dwelling in.

ȧri   dwelling at or with.

ḥeri   dwelling upon.

χeri   dwelling under.

ṭepi   dwelling upon.

χenti   occupying a front position.

These are formed from the prepositions ⟨owl⟩ m, ⟨⟩
r, ḥer, χer, ṭep, and χent respec-

tively. The following examples will illustrate the use
of prepositions :—

I. 1.

en	*ka*	*en*	*Ausâr*	*ân*	*Ani*
To the	ka (double)	of	Osiris,	the scribe	Ani.

2.

paut	*neteru*	*em*	*hennu*	*en*
The company of the gods	[are]	in	praises	because

uben-k

thou risest.

3.

ta	*em*	*sertu*	*en*	*maa*	*satet-k*
The earth [is] in		rejoicing	at the sight	of thy beams.

II. 1.

uben-f	*em*	*χut*	*ảbtet*	*ent*	*pet*
He riseth	in	the horizon	eastern	of heaven.

2.

utâu	*pet*	*ta*	*em*	*mâχait*
Weighers of heaven and earth	in	scales.

3.

   maa - nȧ   *Ḥeru*   *em*   *ȧri*   *ḥemu*

May I see Horus {as the guardian of} the rudder.
                           i. e., standing at

4.

   qem - f   *em*   *χet*   *buṭ*

May it be found on the wood of the table of offerings.

5.

   nuk   *uȧ*   *em*   *ennu*   *en*   *enen*   *neteru*

I [am] one of those gods.

6.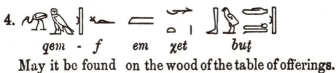

   ȧ   *uȧ*   *pesṭ*   *em*   *Ȧȧḥ*   *pert*

Hail One shining from the Moon! Cometh forth

   Ȧusȧr   *Ani*   *pen*   *em*   *ȧśt - k*

Osiris Ani this among thy multitude.

7.

   em   *hamemet*   *un - nȧ*

In the state of the *hamemet* beings may I lift up my legs

   unun   *Ȧusȧr*

[as] doth lift up the legs Osiris.

8.
án	χenṭ - á	her - f	em	tebt - á
Not let me walk		upon it	with	my sandals.

9.
em	ṭept - re		pert	em
Conformably to the utterance [which] came forth from				

re	ḥen	en	Ḥeru
the mouth of the majesty of			Horus.

III. 1.
áu-f	her	šemi	em - sa	naif
He		followed	after	his

áaut	er	seχet
cattle	in	the fields.

2.
er	paif	per	er	tennu
Into	his	house	at	each

ruha
evening.

3.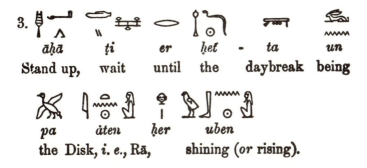

āḥā	ṭi	er	ḥeṭ	-	ta	un
Stand up,	wait	until	the		daybreak	being

pa	āten	ḥer	uben
the Disk, *i. e.*, Rā,		shining (*or* rising).	

4.

ḥept	-	tu	Maāt	er	trāui

Embraced art thou by Maāt at the two seasons.

5.

entek	setemet	er	ānχui-k

Thou hearest with thy two ears.

6.

em	āḥā	er-ȧ	em	meter
Let none	stand up	against me	in	evidence,

em	χesef	er-ȧ	em	taȧat
none make opposition to me		among	the chiefs.	

7.

men	ȧb - k	er	āḥāu - f

Stable is thy heart by (*or* on) its supports.

8.

seχem - à   *em*   *utu*

I have gained the mastery   of   what was commanded

àrit   *er - à*   *ṭep*   *ta*

to be done for me upon earth.

IV. 1.

Teḥuti   *Maāt*   *ḥer*   *āui - f*

Thoth and Maāt upon his two hands (*i. e.*, on the right and left).

2.

ṭā - k   *maa-tu*   *ḥer*   *ṭep*   *ṭuait*

Thou lettest be seen thyself at { the head of the morning, *i. e.*, the early morning, }

hru   *neb*

each   day.

3.

āḥā   *āḥa - nef*   *ḥer - s*

He hath fought   for   it.

4.

āq - sen   *er*   *àsi - à*   *seš - sen*   *ḥer - f*

They enter into my sepulchre, [or] they pass by it.

5.

  i-á *nek* *áθi* *neb - á* *her*

I have come to thee, O Prince, my lord, for the sake

Bent-enθ-reśt

of Bent-enth-resht.

V. 1.

 ár *ḳert* *reχ* *re* *pen* *semaāχeru-*

 If now be known chapter this he will be **made**

 f *pu* *ṭep* *ta* *em Neter-χert*

victorious upon earth [and] in the underworld.

2. *maa-á* *neferu-k* *uṭa - á* *ṭep* *ta*

I shall see thy beauties, I shall be strong upon earth.

VI. 1. *áp* *en* *pa* *ser* *en* *Beχten* *iu*

An envoy of the Prince of Bekhten hath come

 χer *ánut* *āśt* *en* *suten ḥemt*

with gifts many for the queen.

2.

reṭiu　　*seqṭeṭ*　*χer*　*ḥen - k*

Vigorous　　is the *seqtet* boat under thy majesty,

satut - k　　　*em*　　*ḥrȧu*

thy beams　[are]　in [their] faces.

3.

qem-en-tu　　*re*　*pen*　*em*　*Χemennu*　*χer*

Was found　chapter　this　in　Hermopolis　under

reṭiu　　*en*　*ḥen*　*en*　*neter*　*pen*

the two feet　of　the majesty　of　god　this.

VII. 1.

ṭeṭ　*ȧn*　*suten*　　*pa*　　*neter*　*ȧa*

Spake　the king,　　the　　god　great

χer　*seru*　　*ḥȧuti*

with　the princes [and]　chiefs.

2.

θes　　*meṭeḥ*　　*χer*　*ḥen*　*en*　*Ṭetȧ*

[I was] girded with the belt under the majesty of　Teta.

3.   χer   ḥen   en   suten net (or bȧt)   Ȧssȧ   ȧnχ

Under the majesty of { the king of the South and North, } Assa, living

tetta   er   neḥeḥ

for ever   [and]   ever.

VIII. 1.   ȧu   qemt - s   mā   ḥent   ḥer   bennut

It is found   by   women with emerald ore (?).

IX. 1.   ȧu-f   er   ḥems   ḥenā   taif

He   sat   with   his

ḥemt   emtuf   surȧ

wife,   he   drank, etc.

2.   teben-k   pet   ḥenā   Rā   maa-k

Thou goest round heaven with Rā,   thou seest

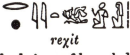

reχit

the beings of knowledge.

3.

àu   sta - tu - f   ḥenā   suteniu

He is led   along   with   the kings of the south,

neti (or bàti)   rā   neb

and the kings of the north   each   day.

X. 1.

ṭua   Rā   χeft   uben - f

Praised be   Rā   when   he riseth.

2.

seqṭeṭ - f   χeft   Rā   er   bu   neḷ

He journeyeth   before   Rā   into   place every

meri - f   àm

wisheth he [to be] there.

3.

àri-à   nek   χut   śetat   em   nut - k

I made for thee a hidden horizon   in   thy city

Uast   χeft   en   āba - k

Thebes   in the face   of   thy courtyard.

XI. 1.

Åmen   *neb*   *nest*   *taui*   *χent*

Amen, lord of the thrones of the world, at the head

Åpt

of the Apts (Karnak).

2.

VI   *pu*   *ḳerθ*   *åm*   *χent*   *mu*

The sixth who is   there is at the head {of the watery abyss.}

XII. 1.

āui - sen   *em*   *sau*   *ḥa´ - k*

Their hands [are] as protectors behind thee.

2.

mest   *tefaut*   *en*   *neteru*

Producer   of the food   of   the gods

ḥa   *karå*

behind   the shrines.

3.

rer - nå   *ḥa*   *suḥt - f*

I go round   behind   his egg.

XIII. 1.

ṭā-tu	nà	ḥetepu	em baḥ	mà
May be given to me	offerings	in the presence	as [to]

šesu	Ḥeru
the followers of Horus.

2.

i -	kuà	χer - ten	ṭer - ten
I have	come	before you, do ye away with

ṭu	neb	àri - à	mà	ennu
evil	all	dwelling in me	like that [which]

àri	en	ten	en	χu	VII	àpu
ye did	for	spirits	seven	these

àmiu	šes	en	neb -	sen
who [are] in the following	of	their	lord

Sepa
Sepa.

XIV. 1.

su	*uār*	*er*	*ḥāt*	*ḥen - f*	*ter*
He	fled	before		his majesty	when

setem - f

he heard [of him].

2.

ṭeḳa - à	*nehaut*	*sentrà*
I planted	sycamores and incense-bearing trees

em	*paik*	*āba*	*bu*
in	thy	courtyard,	never

petrà	*-*	*u*	*ān*	*ter*	*reku neter*
were seen [such as]		they	going back	since	{ the time of the god. }

3.

àm - à	*às*	*ta*	*en*	*ḥeqt*	*ses à*
I have eaten,	behold,	bread	of	sorrow,	I have drunk

mu	*em*	*àb*	*ter*	*hru*	*pef*
water	of	affliction	since	day	that

setem-k   ren - å

[in which] thou didst hear my name.

Examples of the words which are like prepositions
are :—

1. åneṭ   ḥrȧ-k   åmi   em   ḥetepu   neb

   Homage   to thee   dweller   in   peace,   lord

āut   åb

of joy   of heart !

2. χā - θȧ   em   neb   Ṭȧṭȧu   em   ḥeq

Thou art crowned as   lord of Tattu, [and] as   prince

åmi   Abṭu

dwelling   in Abydos.

3. sefeχ - nȧ   åsfet   ȧrt - θen

  I have set free   the faults   which dwell in you.

4.

ṭer - f	nek	ṭut	ȧri
He hath done away	for thee	the evils	dwelling

ḥȧu - k	em	χu	ṭep - re - f
in thy members	by the power of his utterance.		

5.

ȧu-f	her	ennu	χeri	pa	sba
He		looked	under	the	door

en	paif	ȧhait
of	his	stable.

6.

i-tu-f	er	seṭer	χeri	pa	āś
He came	to	lie down	under	the	{cedar tree.}

7.

nuk	χenti	Re - stau
I am	at the head	of Re-stau.

8.

nuk	ka	em	χenti	seχet
I am	the bull	at	the head	of the field.

The following are compound prepositions with examples which illustrate their use.

1. ⟨hieroglyphs⟩ *em ȧsu* in consequence of, in recompense for.

⟨hieroglyphs⟩
ṭā - nef   *ḥeq·ȧ*   *Qemt*   *Ṭeśert*   *em*

He hath granted me to rule Egypt and the desert   in

⟨hieroglyphs⟩
ȧsu   *ȧri*
reward   therefor.

2. ⟨hieroglyphs⟩ *em āq* in the middle.

⟨hieroglyphs⟩
tut   *en*   *Fa-ā*   *em*   *āq*   *ḥāti - f*

An image of the god Fa-ā in the middle of his breast.

3. ⟨hieroglyphs⟩ *em āb* or ⟨hieroglyphs⟩ *em ābu* opposite.

⟨hieroglyphs⟩
ȧu   *ȧpu - nef*   *ȧuset-f*   *em*   *ābu*
Is ordered   for him his seat   opposite

⟨hieroglyphs⟩
sebau
the stars.

4 *em uā* alone.

āḥā	*ser*	*em*	*uā*	*seṭi*	*ses*
Stood	the prince	alone,		he drew the bolt.	

5. *em uaḥ ḥer* in addition to.

ki	*sa*	*ȧmθ*	*ȧbu*	*em*	*uaḥ ḥer*
Another	order	among the priests		in addition to	

sa	*IV*

the orders four [already existing].

6. *em baḥ* before, in the presence of.

seśep	*sennu*	*em baḥ - k*
The receiving of cakes		before thee.

āḥā	*en*	*sen*	*seft*	*em baḥ - ā neteru*
They were		slain		before the gods

7. *emmā* with, among.

er	ȧrit	mert - f	ṭep	ta	emmā
To do		his will	upon	earth	among

ānχiu
the living

8. *em mȧtet* likewise.

em	mȧtet	emtuk	i - nek	er
Likewise		thou	come	to

seχet	χeri	pertu
the fields	with	grain.

9. *em ʀer* about, around.

qeṭ	θesem	ur	em	ȧrit	en ḥemut	er
Building	a bastion	great	with	work	of artificer	by the

χet	ȧter	em	ʀer	ȧbtet
work	of the river	about		the eastern side.

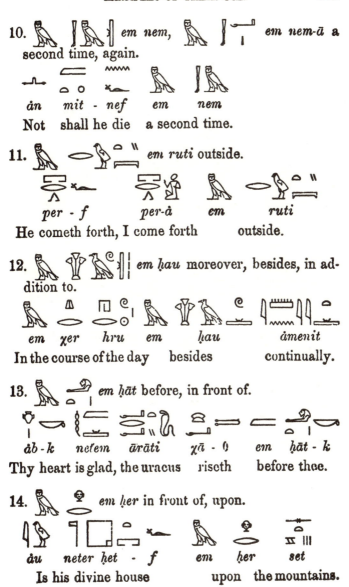

10. 〔hieroglyphs〕 *em nem,* 〔hieroglyphs〕 *em nem-ā* **a** second time, again.

〔hieroglyphs〕

ȧn mit - nef   em   nem

Not shall he die a second time.

11. 〔hieroglyphs〕 *em ruti* outside.

〔hieroglyphs〕

per - f   per-ȧ   em   ruti

He cometh forth, I come forth   outside.

12. 〔hieroglyphs〕 *em ḥau* moreover, besides, in addition to.

〔hieroglyphs〕

em   χer   hru   em   ḥau   ȧmenit

In the course of the day   besides   continually.

13. 〔hieroglyphs〕 *em ḥāt* before, in front of.

〔hieroglyphs〕

ȧb - k   nefem   ārāti   χā - 0   em   ḥāt - k

Thy heart is glad, the uræus   riseth   before thee.

14. 〔hieroglyphs〕 *em her* in front of, upon.

〔hieroglyphs〕

ȧu   neter ḥet - f   em   her   set

Is his divine house   upon the mountains.

15. ⬭ 𓊖 𓏏 *em ḥer âb* within, in the midst of.

aâ	*Nibinaitet*	*enti*	*em*	*ḥer*
The island	of Cyprus	which [is] in the midst		

âb	*Uat -*	*ur*
of the Green great (*i. e.,* the sea)		

16. ⬭ ● ⌐ *em χem* without.

uaḥ	*ka-f*	*ân*	*ârit-â*	*em*
{ He *i. e.,* God }	hath placed his *ka* [in me],	not	do I work	

χem - f	
without him.	

17. 𓅭 𓄿 *em χennu* within, inside.

âuset	*f*	*em*	*χennu*	*kekiu*
His seat is		within		the darkness.

18. *e.n χer* among.

àu   erṭā - sen   per   hi

May it be granted to them   to come forth advancing

em . χer   ḥesu   ent   Àusàr

among   the favoured ones of Osiris.

19. *em χet* after, behind, in the train of.

àu - f   āq - f   em χet   pert   em

He shall enter in   after   coming forth from

neter χert   ent   Àmentet   neſert

the underworld of   Amentet the beautiful.

20. *em sa* after, behind, at the back of.

sàti   Śu   iu   em   sa - k

The slayers   of Shu   come   at thy back

er   ḥesq   ṭep - k

to   cut off   thy head.

21.   *em qeb* among, in the company of.

| *un - nȧ* | *em* | *qeb* | *ḥesi* | *emmȧ* |

Let me live in the company of the favoured ones among

ȧmaχiu

the venerable ones.

22.   *em qeṭ* around, in the circuit of.

| *qeṭ - ȧ* | *sebti* | *em* | *qeṭ - s* |
| I built a | wall | round | about it. |

| *unen* | *bes* | *ȧśt* | *em* | *qeṭeṭ - f* | *neb* |

There shall be flames many   round about it   every
[where] (*i. e.,* throughout).

23.   *em ṭep* upon.

| *paut* | *neteru* | *nek* | *em* | *ṭep* | *mast* |

{ The company } of the gods are to thee upon [their] legs
(*i. e.,* they are standing or kneeling).

24. *em ţebu* in return for.

ȧri - nef   mȧtet   emχet   menȧnȧu-

{ Shall be done } for him the like after   his death

f   em   ţebu   ȧru   ȧri - nef   nȧ

in return for the things which he hath done for me.

25. *em ţer* because of.

ȧn   reχ - f   tai   er   pa

Not   knew he [how] to cross   over   to

enti   paif   sen   serȧu   ȧm   em ţer

where [was] his   brother younger there because of

na   en   emseḥu

the   crocodiles.

ȧu-f   remi   em   terti

Was he   weeping   because of

petrâ	paif	sen	šerâu
the sight of	his	brother	younger.

26. ⸺ er âmtu between (also ⸺ and ⸺).

teχenui	em	smu	benbenet	-	sen
Two obelisks	of	smu metal	their pyramidions		

âbχu	em	ḥert	em	ânit
piercing		upwards	in	the colonnade

šepset	er	âmtu	beχenti	urti	en
noble		between	the two pylons	great	of

suten	ka	neχt
the king,	the bull	mighty.

27. ⸺ er âuṭ between.

âu	pa	tut	en	pa	suten
Was	the	statue	of	the	king

āḫā	ḥer	pai	utu	åu	paif
standing by	the	stele	was		his

Ꮎesemu   er   åuṯ   reṯu - f

greyhound   between   his legs.

28. *er āq* opposite.

åu-f	ḥer	āḫā	ḥer	set	er	āq
He was		standing on the mountain				opposite

ta	nebṯ	šenti	enti	em	pa	mu
the	lock	of hair which [was] in			the water	

29. *er ḳes* by the side of.

ṯā - k	nå	åuset	em	neter- χert	er
Grant thou	to me	a place	in the underworld		by

ḳes   nebu   maāt

the side of the lords   of Maāt.

30. *er bu-n-re* outside, at the place of the door of the way.

àu-f   teṭ - nes - set   em   àri   per
He said   to her,   Do not make an appearance

er   bu - n - re   tem   pa
   outside   so that not   the

imā   her   àṭa - t
sea   seize   thee.

31. *àrmā* with.

na   māṭaiu   en   pa   χer
The   guards   of   the cemetery

enti   àrmā - u
which [were] with them.

32. *er enti* because, so that.

er   enti   betau   ur   ḍa   pa
Because   an evil   very   great   was that

àru   na   meru   set   ḥenā   na

which had done the governors of the lands towards the

seru   en   Āa-perti   ānχ   uᵈa   senb

chiefs   of Pharaoh,   life!   strength!   health!

33. ⬭ er ḥāt before.

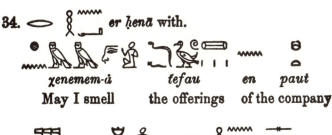

emtuf   àn   naif   àaut

He   brought   his   cattle

er   ḥāt - f

before him.

34. ⬭ er ḥenā with.

χenemem-à   tefau   en   paut

May I smell   the offerings   of the company

neteru   ḥems   er   ḥenā - sen

of the gods,   may I sit down   with   them.

35. ⟨glyphs⟩, ⟨glyphs⟩ *er ḥer* in addition to, over and above.

⟨glyphs⟩

| *er* | *ḥer* | *śetai* | *ṭeṭu* |

In addition to the mysteries recited.

36. ⟨glyphs⟩ *er χet* after, behind

⟨glyphs⟩

| *en* | *ta* | *ḥet* | *Usr-maāt-Rā meri Amen* |
| Of | the | house of king | Usr-maāt-Rā meri Amen |

⟨glyphs⟩

| *er* | *χet* | *pa* | *neter ḥen* | *ṭep* | *en* | *Ámen* |
| after | | the | prophet | chief | of | Amen. |

37. ⟨glyphs⟩ *er χer* with.

⟨glyphs⟩

| *perer* | *er χer* | *hau* |
| Coming forth | with | men and women of the time. |

38. ⟨glyphs⟩ *er śaā* as far as, until.

⟨glyphs⟩

| *smen* | *ḥetepet à* | *maāu* | *en* | *ka-à* |
| Establishing | my offerings | due | to | my ᴋᴀ, |

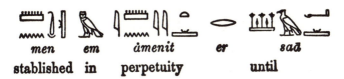

men   em   ȧmenit   er   saȧ

stablished   in   perpetuity   until

neḥeḥ

eternity.

set   uṭa   set   χui   māki   er

They are safe, they are protected [and] guarded

saȧ   ḥeḥ

until   eternity.

39. er sa after, at the back of.

re   en   āq   er   sa   pert

Chapter   of   going in   after   coming forth.

40. ḥer ȧb in, within, among, interior.

ḥā   erek ḥer ȧb   uȧa   -   k

There is rejoicing to thee   in   thy boat,

qet - k   em   ḥetepu
thy sailors   are content.

em ȧmentet em ȧbtet em   tauu   ḥer ȧbu
In the west, in the east, in the countries interior.

ȧneḟ   ḥrȧ - k   Rȧ   neb   maȧt
Homage   to thee,   Rȧ,   lord   of right,

ȧmen   karȧ - f   neb   neteru
hidden   is his shrine,   lord   of the gods,

χeperȧ   ḥeri-ȧb   uta - f
Khepera   in   his boat.

41. ⊙ ⌐ ḥer ȧ at once, straightway.

ȧḥȧ   en   un - en - sen   ḥer ȧ   ȧq
They opened   the gates   at once, entered

en   ḥen-f   er   χennu   en   nut
his majesty   into   the   city.

42. ḥer baḥ before.

ḥetem	em	baḥ	ȧpitu-f	ḥer	baḥ
Destroyed		before	his judgment	[and]	before

qennu-f
his punishment.

43. ḥer mā by

ȧri	-	en	-	θu	enen	ḥer	mā
Done		·		was	this		by

mest	ṯu	· em	nub	er	āu-f
casing	the mountain	in	gold	all	of it.

44. ḥer χer beneath.

seqebeb	-	ȧ	ḥer	χeru	nehet	-	ȧ
May I cool myself			under		my sycamores,

ȧm-ȧ	ṯau	en	ṯāṯā	-	sen
may I eat	cakes	of	their		giving.

45. ☥ 𓎨 *ḥer sa* besides, in addition to, moreover, after.

na	en	*meṭet*	*enti*	*ḥer*	*sa*	*ta*
The		words	which are	after *or* in addition to [those of]		the

useχt	*maāti*
Hall	of Maāti.

àr	*ḥer sa*	*àri - à*	*àru*	*nu*
	After	I had performed	the ceremonies of	

ṭep renpit ḥeb	*uṭen - à*	*en*	*tef*	*Āmen*
the New-Year festival	I made an offering to		father	Amen.

46. ☥ *ḥer ḳes* by the side of.

erṭā - f	*meṭet*	*ḥer*	*ḳes*	*àri*
He giveth	speech	by	the side of theirs.

47. *χer ā* under the hand of, subordinate to.

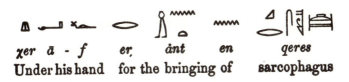

χer	ā - f	er	ȧnt	en	qeres
Under his hand		for the bringing of			sarcophagus

pen	em	Re-au
this	from	Re-au (*i. e.*, Mount Ṭura).

48. χer ḥāt before, in olden time.

Amen - Rā	suten	neteru	pautti
Amen-Rā,	king	of the gods	{ of the two companies[1] }

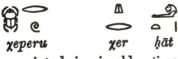

χeperu		χer	ḥāt

[who] came into being in olden time.

49. ter ā at once.

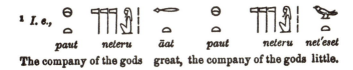

ḥunnu	nefer	māȧ	er	per - k	ter ȧ
Boy	beautiful	come	to	thy house	at once!

[1] *I. e.,*

paut	neteru	āat	paut	neteru	net'eset
The company of the gods		great,	the company of the gods		little.

50. *ter baḥ* from of old, before.

àn	*sep*	*àrit*	*àaut*	*ten*	*en*
Never	was	made {*i. e.,* conferred}	dignity	this	on

bak	*neb*	*ter baḥ*
servant	any	before.

speru	*ṭi*	*erek*	*ter*	*em*	*baḥ*
Coming forth	waiting	for thee		from	of old.

51. *ter enti,*   *ter entet* because.

seḥuā	*renput-sen*	*setekennu*	*àbeṭ-*
Disturbing	their years,	they invade	their months

sen	*ter enti*	*àru*	*en*	*sen*	*ḥet*
because		they	have	done	evil

àmen	*em*	*àrit*	*nek*	*neb*
secretly	in [their]	work	against thee	all.

ter *entet* *ren* *en* *Rā* *em* *χat*
Because the name of Rā [is] in the body

en *Ảusảr*
of Osiris.

ter *entet - f* *em* *uā* *emmā* *ennu*
Because he is as one among those

ảu *χefti - f* *ţer* *em* *śenit*
whose enemies are destroyed by the divine chiefs.

ter *entet* *maa* *su* *neteru* *χu*
Because see him the gods, and spirits,

metu *em* *ảru* *en*
and dead in the forms of

Χenti *-* *Ảmenti*
the Governor of Amentet (*i. e.*, Osiris).

CHAPTER XI.

CONJUNCTIONS AND PARTICLES.

The principal conjunctions are :—

⌇	*en*	because of
⬯	*er*	until
☥	*ḥer*	because
⌇	*χeft*	when
⌇	*mȧ*	as
⬯	*re pu*	or
⌇⌇	*ȧs*	}
⌇⌇	*ȧst*	when
⌇⌇	*ȧsk*	}
•	*χer*	now
⬯		
⌇⬯	*ȧr*	}
⌇⬯	*ȧref*	now, therefore
⬯	*eref*	}

PARTICLES.

Interrogative particles are :

𓄿 *ȧn*, which is placed at the beginning of a sentence and is to be rendered by "?"

	ȧχ	what ?
	nimȧ	who ?
	ȧqeset, or *aśeset*, who ? what ?
	tennu	where ?
	peti	} what ?
	petrȧ	

Negative particles are :—

or	*ȧn*	not
	ȧn sep	at no time, never
	bu	not
	ben	not
	tem	not
	ȧm	not.

Examples of the use of these are :—

1.

neṭer ḥen	re	pu	uā	ȧm-0	ābu
A prophet	or		oṇc	among the priests.	

ȧr	reẋ	śāt (?)	ten	ḥer ṭep	ta	ȧu-f
If	be known	book	this	upon	earth,	he

ȧri - s	em	ānu	ḥer	qeres	re	pu
doeth it	in	writing	upon	a bandage	or	

ȧu-f	per-f	em	hru	neb	mer-f
he	shall come forth		day	every	he pleaseth.

2.

ȧs	ḥen-f	em	Neher	mȧ
When	his majesty [was]	in	Mesopotamia	according

entā-f	θennu	renpit
to his custom	each	year.

ást   ḥen-f   ḥer   T'ah   em   utit-f

When his majesty [was] at   Tchah   in his expedition

sent   ent   neχt

second   of   victory.

ásk   ḥen-f   em   Uast   ḥent

When his majesty [was] in   Thebes,   the mistress

nut   ḥer   árit   ḥes   en   tef   Ámen-Rā

of cities, to do what things pleased father Amen-Rā,

neb   nest   taui   em   ḥeb-f

the lord of the thrones of the world, in   festival

nefer   en   áp   reset

his beautiful of   the temple southern.

3.   án   áu   ḳer - nek   er - s

Shall it be that thou wilt be silent   about it?

àn   *àu*   *àn*   *qebḥ*   *àb*   *en*   *ḥen - k*

Is it   that   not will cool the heart of thy majesty

em   *enen*   *àri - nek*   *ᴣr-à*

at   this that thou hast done to me ?

àn   *àu - ten*   *reꭓ - tini*   *erentet*   *tuà*

Is it   that   ye   know not   that   I even

reꭓ - kuà   *ren*   *en*   *àaṭet*

I know   the name of   the net ?

4.   *ṭeṭ - en - sen*   *àn*   *ḥen-f*   *entu-*

Said   to them   his   majesty,   "Ye [are]

ten   *àꭓ*

what (or who) ?"

Iꮶaṭāi   *em*   *màtet*   *su*   *mà*   *àꭓ*

The country of Iꮶaṭāi in likeness is it like what ?

pa	ṭemȧt	en	χirebu	ḥer
The	town	of	Aleppo	in

taif	merṭareȧat	pai-
its	neighbourhood [and]	its

f	χet	mȧ	ȧχ
	ford [is]	like	what?

5.

un - nȧ	nimā	trȧ	tu	entek
Open to me!	Who	then		art thou?

nuk	uȧ	ȧm	ten	nimā	enti
I am	one	of	you.	Who	is

ḥenā - k
with thee?

ȧu - set	ḥer	ṭeṭ - nef	ementek	en
She		said unto him,	"Thou art ..	

nimā   *trā*
who   then ?"

6. *ānχ - k*   *āref*   *em*   *āseset*   *χer*
Thou wilt live   then   on   what   with

sen   *neteru*
them the gods ?

āseset   *pu*   *χu*   *pui*   *sem*
What is   spirit   that [which] goeth

her   *χat-f*   *peḥti - fi*   *θes-f*
upon   his belly, [and] his two thighs, [and] his back ?

ā *Teḥuti* *āseset* *pu* *χepert* *set* *em*
O Thoth, what   háth happened to them,

mesu   *Nut*
the children of Nut ?

à	Tem	àšeset	pu	šas - à
O	Temu	{what kind of place is this}		I have journeyed

er	set
into	it ?

àšeset	pu	àḥā	em	ānχ
What is		[my] duration	in	life ?

(i. e., How long shall I live ?)

7.

erṭā	nek	un - k	teni
Shall be given to thee		thy food	where ?

.... - sen	neteru	er-à
Say	they, the gods,	unto me.

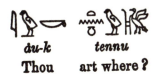

àu-k	tennu
Thou	art where ?

8.

nuk	mȧu	pui	peśeni
I am	cat	that	the fighter (?)

ȧśeṭ	er	ḳes - f	em	Ȧnnu
of the persea tree	by	its side	in	Annu

ḳerḥ	pui	en	ḥetem	χefti
night	that	of the destruction	of the enemies	

nu	Neb-er-ṭer	ȧm-f	peti	eref
of	Neb-er-tcher	in it.	What	then is

su	mȧu	pui	ṭa	Rā	pu	ṭesef
it ?[1]	Cat	that	male	Rā	is	himself.[2]

peti	eref	su	An-ȧ-f	pu
What then is		it ? The god An-ā-f	is it	

(*i. e.*, it refers to An-ā-f).

---

[1] *I. e.*, What is the explanation of this passage?

[2] *I. e.*, That male cat is Rā himself.

petrá — What [is]   *ren - k* — thy name   *án*   *sen* — [say] they   *er-á* — to me?

petrá — What   *maat - nek* — didst thou see   *ám* — there?

petrá — What didst [say] thou   *án - k*   *en* — to   *sen*   *áu* — them? I have   *maa-* — seen

ná   *áhehii* — rejoicings   *em* — in   *ennu* — these   *en*   *taiu* — lands

Fenχu — of the Fenkhu.

petrá — What   *ertá - en - sen* — did they give   *nek* — thee?   *besu* — A flame

pu   *en* — of   *seśet* — fire,   *ḥená*   *uaṭ* — and a tablet   *en* — of   *θeḥent* — crystal.

petrà	àref	àrit	nek	eres	àu
What	then didst thou	with	it [them]?	I

qeres	-	nà	set	ḥer	uteb	en
buried			them	by the	furrow	of

Mããat	em	χet	χaiu
Mããat	as	things	for the night.

petrà	qemt	-	nek	ḥer - f	uteb
What	didst thou find			by it,	the furrow

Māat	uas	pu	ṭes	erṭà
of Māat?	A sceptre	flint,	'Giver

nifu	ren - f
of winds'	is its name.

petrà	àref	àrit -	nek	er	pa
What	then	didst	thou	with	the

bes   en   seśet   ḥenā   pa   uaṭ   en
flame   of   fire   and   the   tablet   of

θeḥent   em - χet   qeres - k   set
crystal   after   thou didst bury them?

àuḥet - nå   ḥer - s   àu   seśeṭ - nå
I said words   over them   I   dug

set   àu   āχem - nå   seśet   àu
it up,   I   extinguished the fire,   I

seṭ - nå   uaṭ   qemamu
broke   the   tablet,   [I] created

en   mer
a pool of water.

9. àn   χesef - f   àn   śenā - f   her
Not   opposed is he,   not   turned back is he at

*sbau   nu   Åmentet

the doors   of the underworld.

ån   åm   åut   meḥit

Not   having eaten   goats [or]   fish.

ån - f   su   må   båau   en

He brought   it   as   a wonderful thing   to

suten   χeft   maa - f   entet   seśeta

the king when   he saw   that [it was] a mystery

pu   åa   ån   maa   ån   petrå

great, [hitherto] not   seen [and]   not   observed.

ån   åu   ḳert   ån   åri - entu

For   not   is it [possible], not   can   be made

neṭem-[t]emit   åm - s

love   in it.

10.   *emmā*   *θet - uȧ em ḥaqet*
  Let   me take possession of   the captives

en   *Ȧusȧr*   *ȧn*   *sep*   *un - ȧ*   *em*
.of   Osiris,   at no time   let me be   among
    (*i. e.*, never)

smait   *Suti*
the fiends   of Suti.

ȧn   *sep*   *pat*   *ȧrit*   *mȧtet*   *en*
Never   before   was done the like   by

bak   *neb*
servant   any.

ȧn   *sep*   *pa*   *mȧtu*   *setem*
Never   before   the like   was heard.

11.   *bu*   *petrȧ - k*   *ta*   *en*   *Ȧupa,*
  Not   hast thou seen the land   of   Aupa? [And]

χaṭumā
of Khatumā

bu rex - k
not knowest thou

qaȧ - f
its form,

Iḳaṭāi
and Iḳaṭāi

em mȧtet su mȧ ȧχ
in resemblance it [is] like what?[1]

bu
Not

ȧru - k
hast thou made

utui
a journey

er
to

Qeṭeš
Kadesh

ḥenā
and

Tubaχet
Tubakhet?

bu
Not

šemi - k
hast thou gone

er na en
to the

šasu
Shasu people

χeri
who have

ta
the

pet
bowmen [and]

māšau,
soldiers?

bu
Not

ṭeḳas - k
hast thou passed over

---

[1] Dost thou not know what kind of place Khaṭumā is, and what sort of land Iḳaṭāi is?

uat	er	Pamaḳare	bu	pui
the way	to	Pamakare ?	Not	did

na	áḥau	reχ	peḥ - f
the	thieves	know [where]	he had arrived.

bu	pu	uā	meṭet	mā-á	ḥeru
Not [any]	one		spake	with me	except

paik	sen	šeráu
thy	brother	younger.

12.

seχa - sen	ren - á	ben	árit
May they mention	my name,	not	making

ābu	em baḥ	nebu	maāt
cessation,[1]	before	the lords	of law.

---

[1] *I. e.,* unceasingly.

ȧs   *ben*   *ȧr*   *em*   *neṭer - uȧ*

When   not   I was working

hab - k   *er*   *ȧn*   *en - n*   *pertu*

thou didst send   to   bring   for   us   grain,

ȧu   *taik*   *ḥemt ḥer feṭ - nȧ*   *māȧi*

was   thy   wife[1] saying to me, 'Come', etc.

13.   *iu-k*   *en - n*   *tem*   *seχau-*

Come thou to   us   not [having] thy memories

k   *iu-k*   *em*   *ȧru - k*

of evil, come thou in   thy form.

tem   *χesef*   *su*   *em*   *at - f*

Not   repelling   him   in   his moment.

---

[1] *I e.*, Was it not when I was working that thou didst send me to fetch grain, [and as I was fetching it] thy wife said to me, 'Come'.

petrȧ	set	tem - k	teṭ
On seeing	it	do not thou	say,

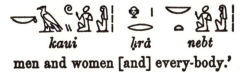

χenś - k	ren - ȧ	en
'Thou hast made to stink	my name	before

kaui	ḥrȧ	nebt

men and women [and] every-body.'

14.

ȧm	ȧq	ȧq	ȧm	per	peru

Not entered a comer in, not came out a comer out,

ȧri	ḥen-f	merer-f
did	his majesty	his will.

ȧḥȧ	en	hab - nef	en	sen	em	teṭ
He sent		to	them,	saying,		

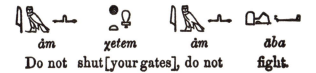

ȧm	χetem	ȧm	ȧba
Do not	shut [your gates], do not		fight.

àm - k   àri   her   em   reθ

Do not   make   terror   in men and women.

àm - f   sàu   erek   er

Let it not [be]   that thou criest   out   against

setemet-k   àm   pu   en   àb

what thou hearest,   that there may not be   a heart

beqbequ

of cowardice (?).

àm-à   ah-à   en   àu

Not shall I   suffer I   overthrow

nest-à   àmt   uàa   en   Rā

from my throne in   the boat   of   Ra

āa

the mighty one.

àm	*erṭā*	*neken*	*er - à*	*àm-*
Do not	cause	injury	to me.	Do not

k	*erṭā*	*ṭep - à*	*ermen*	*àm - à*
thou	cause	my head	to fall away	from me.

àm - k	*àri*	*ḥer*	*ḥrà nebt*	*àpu*	*ḥer*
Do not thou perform	[it]	before	people,	but	only

ḥāu - k	*tes-k*
thine own	self.

EXTRACTS FOR READING.

I. From an inscription of Pepi I.
[VIth dynasty.] .

111.

ha	Pepi	pu	ár	seθes	-	θu
Hail	Pepi	this!		Rise up		thou,

112.

áḥā	uāb - k	uāb
stand up !	Pure art thou,	pure is

ka - k	uāb	ba-k	uāb
thy double,	pure is	thy soul.	pure is

seχem - k	i - nek	mut-k	i - nek
thy power.	Cometh to thee	thy mother,	cometh to thee

Nut	šenem	urt	s - uāb - s	θu	Pepi

Nut, the fashioner great, she purifieth thee, O Pepi

pu	šenem - s	θu		113.	Pepi	pu

this, she fashioneth thee   Pepi   this,

χu	ås	ku-k	ha	Pepi	pu

protecting when thou movest. Hail Pepi   this,

uāb - t	uāb	ka - k	uāb

pure art thou, pure is thy double, pure is

seχem - k	åm	χu	uāb

thy power among the spirits, pure is

ba-k	åm	neteru	ha	114.	Pepi	pu

thy soul among the gods. Hail   Pepi   this,

āåab - nek	qesu - k	sešep-nek	ṭep-k

are brought to thee thy bones, thou receivest thy head

χer	Seb	åter-f	ṭut	årt - k
before	Seb;	he destroyed the evil belonging to thee

Pepi	pu	χer	Tem
Pepi	this	before	Tem.

The above passage is an address made to the dead king Pepi by the priest which declares that he is ceremonially pure and fit for heaven. The *ka, ba* and *sekhem,* were the "double" of a man, his soul, and the power which animated and moved the spiritual body in heaven; the entire economy of a man consisted of *khat* body, *ka* double, *ba* soul, *khaibit* shadow, *khu* spirit, *åb* heart, *sekhem* power, *ren* name, and *sāḥu* spiritual body. The reference to the bringing of the bones seems to refer to the dismemberment of bodies which took place in pre-dynastic times, and the mention of the receiving of the head refers to the decapitation of the dead which was practised in the earliest period of Egyptian history. Nut was the mother of the gods and Seb was her husband; Tem or Temu was the setting sun, and, in funeral texts, a god of the dead.

II. Funeral Stele of Panehesi.

(Brugsch, *Monuments de l'Égypte*, Plate 3.)
[XIXth dynasty.]

1.

ṭuau	*Rā*	*χeft*	*ḥetep-f*	*em*
Adoreth	Rā	when	he setteth	on

χut	*ȧmentet*	*ent*	*pet*	*ȧn*	*uā*	*ȧqer*
the horizon	western	of	heaven	the one perfect,		

ȧn	*utḥu*	*en*	*suten*	*ȧpt*	*Pa-neḥesi*
the scribe of	{the table of offerings}	of the royal house,			Pa-neḥesi,

teṭ - f	*ȧneṭ - ḥrȧ-k*	*Rā*	*ȧri*
[and] he saith :—	Homage to thee,	O Rā,	maker

2.

tememu	*Tem Ḥeru-χuti*	*neter uā*
of mortals,	Temu-Harmachis,	god one,

ānχ	em	maāt	ári	enti
living	upon	right and truth,	maker of	things that are,

qemam	unenet	en	álu
creator	of {things which shall be,}	[and] of	animals,

reθ	pert	em	maat-f	neb
[and] of {men and women,}	who come forth	from	his eye.	Lord

pet	neb	ta	ári	χeru
of heaven,	lord of earth,		maker of beings terrestrial [and]	

ḥeru	Neb-er-ter	ka	em
of { beings celestial,}	Neb-er-tcher,	the bull	of

paut neteru	suten	ḥert	neb	neteru
{the company of the gods,}	king	of heaven,	lord of the gods,

áθi	her	paut neteru	neter	netri
prince,	chief of	{the company of the gods,}	god	divine

5. χeper tesef   pauti

self-created,   god of the two companies of the gods

χeper	em	ḥāt	hennu - nek

coming into being in the beginning. Praises are to thee,

ári	neteru	Tem	seχeper	reχit

O {maker of the gods,} Temu making to exist   mankind,

neb	benerát	āa	mert
lord	of sweetness,	great	of love;

pest - f	ānχ	ḥrá nebt	ṭā-á	nek
he shineth [and]	live	mankind.	I give	to thee

7. ἀaiu   em   māśer   seḥetep-á

praises   at   eventide, I make thee to set

tu   ḥetep·k   em   ānχ   åu   sektet

[when] thou settest   in   life.   The *sektet* boat

ḥer   seau   åṭet   em   ahi

is glad,   the *åṭet* boat is   in   joyful

ḥennu   nemå - sen   nek   Nu[t]

praising [as]   they journey to thee.   The goddess Nut

em   ḥetep   qet - k   ḥåå - θå   seχer

is at peace,   thy sailors are rejoicing;   hath over-

en   χut - k   χefti - k

thrown   thine eye   thine enemy.

neḥem   reṭ   ent   Āpep   ḥetep - k

Carried away are the leg[s] of   Āpep.   Thou settest,

nefer   åb - k   au   em   χut   ent   Manu.

glad is thy heart joyful   in   the horizon of   Manu.

seḥet - k   ȧm   en   neter nefer neb
Thou makest light there,   god beautiful, lord

ḥeḥ   ḥeq   Aukert   11.   ṭā - k
of eternity, prince   of Aukert.   Thou givest

seśep   en   enti   ȧm   xefti
thy radiance upon those there, [thy] enemies

ṭekai - sen   neferu-k   em   ...... sen
    see   thy beauties in their [abodes and]

em   tephetu - sen   āui - sen   em
in their habitations [and] their   hands

ȧaui   en   ka - k   ȧmentiu   em
adore   thy double; the beings in Amenti

ḥāātu   13.   emxet   eref   peṣt-k
rejoice   after   thou hast shone

en   *sen*   *nebu*   *ṭuat*   *åbu - sen*

upon   them,   the lords of the underworld their hearts

neṭem   *seḥeṭ - k*   *Amentet maat - sen*

are glad [when] thou lightest up Amentet. Their eyes

14.

seśu   *en*   *maa - k*   *χenteś*

open widely   at   the sight of thee,   refreshed

åbu - sen   *maa - sen*   *tu*   *ḥaa*

are their hearts [when] they see   thee ;   rejoiceth

15.

ṭet - k   *ḥer*   *sen*   *ån*   *meni*   *mestu*

thy body through them. Without pain [are] the births

neteɣ   *ḥau - sen*   *entek*   *meses-*

of god [which are] their members ; thou   givest birth

set   *er*   *au*   *uben - k*   *ṭer - k*

to them, all of them.   Thou risest, thou destroyest

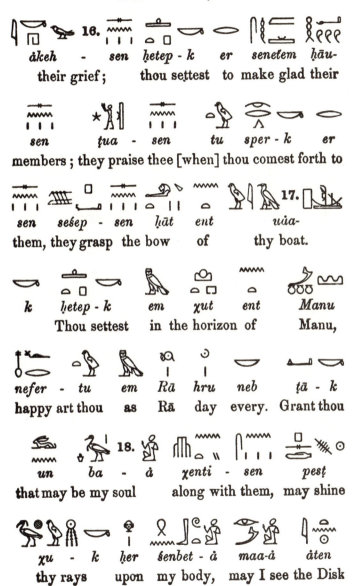

åkeh   - sen   ḥetep - k   er   senetem   ḥāu-
their grief;   thou settest   to   make glad their

sen   ṭua - sen   tu   sper - k   er
members; they praise thee [when] thou comest forth to

sen   seśep - sen   ḥāt   ent   uåa-
them, they grasp   the bow   of   thy boat.

k   ḥetep - k   em   χut   ent   Manu
Thou settest   in the horizon of   Manu,

nefer - tu   em   Rā   hru   neb   ṭā - k
happy art thou   as   Rā   day   every.   Grant thou

un   ba - å   χenti - sen   pesṭ
that may be my soul   along with them,   may shine

χu - k   ḥer   śenbet - å   maa-å   åten
thy rays   upon   my body,   may I see the Disk

19.

χeft   enen   χu   àqeru nu neter-χert

[being] opposite to those spirits   perfect of the underworld

ḥemsiu   embaḥ   Un-nefer   20.   àriu

who sit in the presence of Un-nefer,   and who make

mā   χeru   en   ka   en Ausàr   ān

. . . . . .   to the double of Osiris, the scribe

uthu   en   suten àpt   Pa-neḥesi

of the table of offerings of the royal house, Pa-neḥesi.

21.

àn   sa - f   seānχ   ren - f

[Dedicated] by   his son, who maketh to live his name,

ān   netert   ent neb   taui

the scribe of the goddess (?) of the lord of the two lands,

setep   sa   àm   ḥet āat   Ȧp-uat-mes   maā-χeru

{ worker of }   in   the palace, Ap-uat-mes   right of speech
{ magic [1] }   (*or* triumphant).

III. Inscription of Ȧnebni.

(Sharpe, *Egyptian Inscriptions*, Plate 56.)

[XVIIIth dynasty.]

1.   àrit   em   ḥeset   netert   nefert   nebt

Made by the favour of the goddess beautiful, lady

taui   Rā-maāt-ka   ānχ-θ   ṭeṭ-θ   Rā

of the two lands,   Ḥātshepset   living, established Rā

mà   ṭetta   ḥenā   sen - s   nefer   neb

like for ever,   and   her brother   beautiful, the lord,

àri   χet   Men-χeper-Rā   ṭā   ānχ   Rā mà

maker of things, Thothmes III.,   giver of life   Rā like

---

[1] Literally, "protecting by means of the 𓏲" which was an object used in performing magical ceremonies.

tetta   3. *suten*   *ṭā*   *ḥetep*   *Ámen*   *neb*   *nest*

for ever.   King give an offering!   Amen,   lord   { of the }
                                                  { thrones }

taui   *Ausár*   *ḥeq*   *tetta*   *Anpu*

of the two lands, [and] Osiris, prince of eternity, Anubis

χent   4. *neter*   *ḥet*   *ȧm*   *Ut*   *neb*

dweller by the divine coffin, dweller in { the city of } lord
                                                     { embalmment, }

Ta-ṭeser   *ṭā - sen*   *per-χeru*   *menχ*

of Ta-tcheser, may they give sepulchral meals,   linen
                                                          garments,

sentrȧ merḥ   5. *χet nebt*   *nefert*   *ābt*   *perert*

incense, wax, thing every beautiful, pure, what appeareth

nebt   *her*   *χaut* - *sen*   6. *em*   *χert*   *hru*

{ of every } upon altar   their during the course of the day
{ kind }

ent	rā	neb		surā	mu	her
of	day	every,	the	drinking	of water	at

betbet	āter	seset	ām	en
the deepest part of the river,	the breathing	there	of the

meht	āq	pert	em	Re-stau	en
north wind,	entrance	and exit	from	Re-stau	to the

ka	en	uā	āqer	hes	en	neter-f	meru
double	of the one	perfect,	favoured of	his god,	loving

neb - f	her	menχ - f	šes
his lord	by reason of	his beneficence,	following

neb-f	er	utut - f	her	set	rest
his lord		on his expeditions	over	the country south

mehti	suten sa	mer	χāu		suten
[and] north,	royal son,	overseer of	the weapons of	the king,

Ånebni *maā-ɣeru* *ɣer* *neteru* *paut*

Anebni right of speech before the gods [and] the company

neteru

of the gods.

IV. Text from the CXXVth Chapter of the Book of the Dead.

[XVIIIth dynasty.]

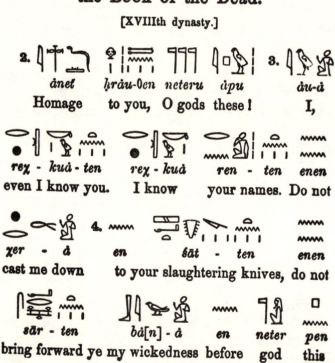

2. *ånet* *ḥrȧu-ben* *neteru* *ȧpu*   3. *ȧu-ȧ*

Homage to you, O gods these !   I,

reɣ - kuȧ - ten   *reɣ - kuȧ*   *ren - ten*   *enen*

even I know you.   I know   your names. Do not

ɣer - ȧ   4. *en*   *šāt - ten*   *enen*

cast me down   to your slaughtering knives, do not

sār - ten   *bȧ[n] - ȧ*   *en*   *neter*   *pen*

bring forward ye my wickedness before   god   this

enti	θen	em χet - f	enen	iu-tu	sep - à
whom	ye	follow him,	let not	come	my moment

ḥer - ten	ṭeṭ - ten	maāt	er - à	embaḥ
before you.	Declare ye	right and truth	for me	before

à	6. Neb-er-ṭer	ḥer	entet	àri - nà
the hand of	Neb-er-tcher,	because		I have done

maāt	em	Ta-merà	en	śen - à
right and truth	in	Ta-mera [Egypt].	Not	have I cursed

neter	en	iu	sep - à	àneṭ	ḥràu-ten
God,	not hath come		my moment.	Homage	to you,

neteru	àm	useχt - θen	ent	7. maāti
O gods	who live in	your hall	of	right and truth,

ati	ḳer	em	χat - sen	ānχiu
without	evil	in	their bodies,	who live

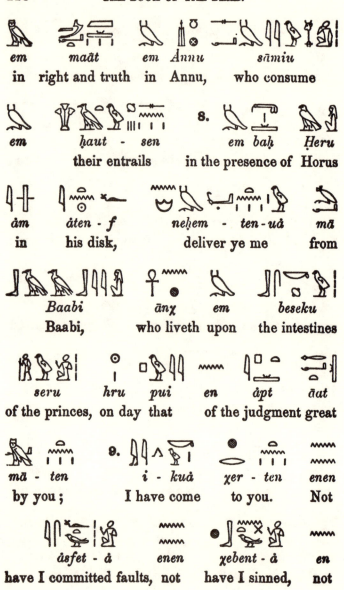

em	*maāt*	*em*	*Annu*	*sāmiu*
in	right and truth	in	Annu,	who consume

em	*ḥaut - sen*	8. *em baḥ*	*Ḥeru*
	their entrails	in the presence of	Horus

ȧm	*ȧten - f*	*neḥem - ten - uȧ*	*mā*
in	his disk,	deliver ye me	from

Baabi	*ānχ em*	*beseku*
Baabi,	who liveth upon	the intestines

seru	*hru*	*pui*	*en*	*ȧpt*	*āat*
of the princes,	on day	that	of the judgment	great

mā - ten	9. *i - kuȧ*	*χer - ten*	*enen*
by you;	I have come	to you.	Not

ȧsfet - ȧ	*enen*	*χebent - ȧ*	*en*
have I committed faults,	not	have I sinned,	not

tu - à   *enen*   *meterɯ - à*   *enen*

have I done evil, not   have I borne false witness, not

àri - nà   *χet*   *eref*   *ānχ - à*   *em*

let be done to me anything therefore. I live   in

10. *maāt*   *sām - à*   *em*   *maāt*

right and truth,   I feed   upon right and truth

àb - à   *àu*   *àri - nà*   *teţet*   *ret*

my heart. I have done that which commanded men,

hereret   *neteru her-s*   *àu*   *se-ḥetep-nuà*   *neter*

are satisfied the gods thereat. I have appeased God

em   *mert*   - *f*   **11.**   *àu*   *erţā - nà*   *tau*

by [doing] his will.   I have given bread

en   *ḥeqet*   *mu*   *en*   *àbi*

to   the hungry, water to   the thirsty,

ḥebs	en	ḥaiu	māχen
clothes	to	the naked,	and a boat

ảui	12.	ảu	ảri - nả	neter-ḥetepu en
to the shipwrecked.		I have made	offerings	to the

neteru	perχeru	en	χu	neḥem-
gods, and	sacrificial meals to	the spirits.		Deliver

ten -	uả	ảr	ten	χu	uả
ye	me	then	ye,	protect	me

ảr	ten	enen	smả - ten	er - ả	em baḳ
then	ye,	not	make accusation ye	against me	before

neter	āa	13.	nuḳ	āb	re	āb	āảiu
the god great.			I am pure of mouth,		pure of hands.		

feṭ - tu - nef	iui	sep sen	ản	maaiu
Is said to him,	Come,	twice,	by	those who see

su	*ḥer entet*	*setem - nå*	*meṭet*	*tui*
him,	because	I have heard	speech	that

ṭeṭet	*en*	*åa*	*ḥenå*	*måu*	*em*
spoken	by	the Donkey	with	the Cat	in

per	*Ḥepṭ-re*	*meteru - å*	*em*
the house of	Hepṭ-re.	I have borne testimony

ḥer - f	*ṭå - f*	*tentu*	*åu*	*maa - nå*
before him,	he hath given the decision.	I have seen

peseś	*åśeṭ*	*em*	*χennu*
the division of the persea trees		within

Re-stau	*nuk*	*semiu - å*	*em baḥ*
Re-stau.	I,	I offer up prayers	in the presence of

neteru	*reχ*	*χert*	*χat - sen*
the gods	knowing	what concerneth	their persons.

i - *nå*	*åa*	*er*	*semeter*
I have come	advancing	to	make a declaration of

maāt	*er*	*erţāt*	16. *åusu*	*er*
right and truth, to	place		the balance	upon

åḥāu - *f*	*em*	*χennu*	*ḳaåu*
its supports	within		the amaranthine bushes.

å	*qa*	*ḥer*	*åat* - *f*	*neb*
Hail	exalted	upon	his standard,	lord

atefu	*åri*	*ren* - *f*	*em*	*neb*
of the *atef* crown,	making	his name	as	the lord

17.
nifu	*neḥem* - *kuå*	*mā*	*naik*
of winds,	deliver me	from	thy

en	*åputat*	*uţeţiu*
	messengers	who make to happen

θemesu   seχeperiu   àṯerit

dire deeds,   who make to arise   calamities,

18.   àt   ṯamet   ent ḥràu-sen

    without   covering   upon their faces,

ḥer entet   àri - nà   maāt   neb

because   I have done   right and truth.   O lord of

maāt   āb - kuà   ḥāti - à   em

right and truth, I am pure,   my breast   is

ābu   peḥi - à   19.   turà   ḥer-àb-à

washed,   my hinder parts are cleansed, my interior

em   seŝeṯit   maāt   enen

[hath been] in   the pool of right and truth, not [is]

āt   àm - à   ŝu   āb - nà   em

a member in me   lacking. I have been purified in

seṣeṭit   reset   ḥetep-nȧ   em   Ḥemt

the pool   southern,   I have rested   in   Hemet,

20.

meḥtet   em   seχet   saneḥemu

to the north   of   the field of   the grasshoppers;

ȧbet   qeti   ȧm - s   em   unnut

bathe   the divine sailors'   in it   at the season of

ḳerḥ   en   senāā   ȧb   en   neteru

night   to   gratify (?)   the heart of   the gods

em   χet   seṣ-ȧ   ḥer-s   em   21.   ḳerḥ

after   I have passed   over it   by   night and

em   hru   ṭāu   iut - f   ȧn - sen   er - ȧ

by day.   They grant   his coming,   they say   to me,

nimā   trȧ   tu   ȧn - sen   er - ȧ

Who   then art   thou?   say they   to me.

pu — trá — ren - k — án - sen — er - á

What — then is — thy name? — say — they — to me.

nuk — ruṭ — χeri — en — ḥait — ámi

I — grow — among — the flowers dwelling in

baaq — ren - á — seś-nek — ḥer mā

the olive tree is — my name. — Pass on thou — forthwith,

án - sen — er - á — seś-ná — ḥer — nut

say — they — unto me. — I have passed — by — the town

meḥtet — baat — peti — trá — maa - nek

north of — the bushes. — What — then — didst thou see

ám — χenṭ — pu — ḥená — mesṭet — peti — trá

there? The leg — and the thigh. — What then

án-k — en — sen — áu — maa - ná — áhehi

didst thou say to — them? — I saw — rejoicing

em	ennu	taiu	Fenχu		peti	trȧ
in	those	lands	of the Fenkhu.		What	then

erṭȧt-sen	nek	24. besu	pu	en	seśet
did give they to thee ?	A flame	it was	of	fire,	

ḥenā	uaṫ	en	θeḥent	peti	trȧ
together with	a tablet	of	crystal.	What	then

ȧri - nek	eres	ȧu	qeres - nȧ	set	ḥer
didst thou do therewith ?		I buried	them	by	

uteb	en	maāti	em	χet	χaui
the furrow of	Maāti	with the things	of the night.		

peti	trȧ	25. qem - nek	ȧm	ḥer	uteb
What	then	didst thou find	there	by the furrow	

en	maāti	uas	pu	en	ṭes	ȧu
of	Maāti ?	A sceptre	of	flint (?) ;		

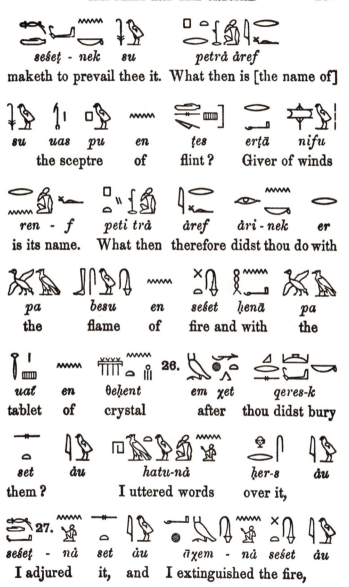

seśeṯ - nek   su   petrå åref

maketh to prevail thee it.   What then is [the name of]

su   uas   pu   en   ṯes   erṯā   nifu

the sceptre   of   flint ?   Giver of winds

ren - f   peti trå   åref   åri - nek   er

is its name.   What then therefore didst thou do with

pa   besu   en   seśet   ḥenā   pa

the   flame   of   fire and with   the

uaṯ   en   θeḥent   **26.** em χet   qeres-k

tablet   of   crystal   after   thou didst bury

set   åu   hatu-nå   ḥer-s   åu

them ?   I uttered words   over it,

27. seśeṯ - nå   set   åu   āχem - nå   seśet   åu

I adjured   it,   and   I extinguished the fire,

seţ - nả   uaţ   em   qemam   28.

I made use of the tablet in   creating

en   mer   māåi   årek   āq   ḥer

a pool of water. Come   then   pass in   over

sba   pen   en   useχt   ten   ent   Mañti

door   this   of   Hall   this   of   Maåti,

29.   åu - k   reχ - 0å - n   enen (i.e., ån)   ţā - å

thou art   knowing us.   Not   will I let

āq - k   ḥer - å   ån   benś   en

enter thee   over me,   saith   the bolt   of

sba   pen   30.   [å]n-ås   ţeţ - nek   ren - å

door   this,   except   thou sayest   my name.

teχ   en   bu   maā   ren - t

Weight of the place of right and truth is thy name.

ȧn   ṭā - ȧ   āq - k   **31.**   ḥer - ȧ   ȧn
Not   will let I   enter thee   by me,   saith

ārit   unem   ent   sba   pen
the post   right   of   door   this,

[ȧ]n-ȧs   ṭeṭ - nek   ren - ȧ   **32.**   ḥenku - nef
except   thou sayest   my name.   He weigheth

fat   maāt   ren·t enen (i.e., ȧn)
the labours of   right and truth   is thy name.   Not

ṭā - ȧ   āq - k   ḥer-ȧ   **33.**   ȧn   ārit
will I let   enter thee   by me,   saith   the post

ȧbet   ent   sba   pen   [ȧ]n-ȧs   ṭeṭ - nek
left   of   door   this,   except thou sayest

ren - ȧ   ḥenku   **34.**   en   ȧrp   ren - t
my name.   Judge   of   wine is thy name.

enen
(*i.e.*, *ȧn*)   *ṭā - ȧ*   *seś - k*   *ḥer - ȧ*   *ȧn*   *sati*

Not   will I let pass thee   over me,   saith the threshold

(*sic*)
en   *sba*   *pen*   **35.** [*ȧ*]*n-ȧs*   *teṭ - nek*   *ren - ȧ*

of   door   this,   except thou sayest   my name.

ȧua   *en*   *Ḳeb*   *ren - k*   *enen* (*i.e.*, *ȧn*)

Ox   of   Ḳeb   is thy name.   Not

36.   *un - ȧ*   *nek*   *ȧn*   *qert*   *ent*

will I open   to thee,   saith   the bolt-socket   of

sba   *pen*   [*ȧ*]*n-ȧs*   *teṭ - nek*   *ren - ȧ*

door   this,   except   thou sayest   my name.

saḥ   **37.**   *en*   *mut - f*   *ren - t*

Flesh   of   his mother   is thy name.

enen (*i.e.*, *ȧn*)   *un - ȧ*   *nek*   *ȧn*   *pait*

Not   will I open to thee, saith   the lock

en   sba   pen [à]n às   teṭ - nek   ren - à
of   door   this, except thou sayest   my name.

ānχet uṭat   ent   Sebek   neb
Liveth the *utchat*   of   Sebek,   the lord of

Baχau   ren-t enen (àn)   un - à
Bakhau,   is thy name. Not   will I open

nek enen(àn) ṭā - à   āq - k   ḥer - à   àn
to thee, not will I let pass thee over me,   saith

àri   āa   en   sba   pen [à]n às
the dweller at the door of   door   this, except

teṭ - nek   ren - à   qebt   Śu   erṭā-nef
thou tellest my name. Arm of Shu   that placeth itself

em   sau   Àusàr   ren - k   enen (àn)
for the protection of Osiris   is thy name.   Not

ṭā - n   *seś - ḳ*   *ḥer - n*   *àn*   *ḥeptu*

will we allow to pass thee   by us,   say   the posts

en   *sba*   *pen*   [*àn*]*às*   *teṭ - nek*   *ren - n*

of   door   this,   except thou sayest   our names.

neχenu   *nu*   *Rennut*   *ren-ten*

Serpent children   of   Rennut are   your names.

àu - k   **40.**   *reχ - θà - n*   *seś*   *àrek*   *ḥer - n*

Thou knowest us,   pass   then   by us.

enen (àn)   *χenṭ - k*   *ḥer - à*   *àn*   *sati*

Not   shalt tread thou   upon me,   saith   the floor

en   *useχt*   *ten*   [*àn*]*às*   *teṭ - k*

of   hall   this,   except thou sayest

ren - à   *ḥer*   *mā*   *àref*   *àu - à*   *ḳert*

my name.   . . . .   I am   silent,

āb - kuā	ḥer entet	**41.** [ā]n	reχ - n
I am pure,	because	not	do we know

reṭ - k	χenṭ - k	ḥer - n	ām - sen
thy two legs	thou treadest	upon us	with them;

ṭeṭ	ārek	nā	set	besu	em baḥ
tell	then	to me	them.	Traveller	before

Amsu	ren	en	reṭ - ā	unemi
Menu (or, Amsu)	is the name	of	my leg	right.

unpet	ent Nebt-ḥet	ren	en	**42.** reṭ - ā
Grief	of Nephthys	is the name	of	my leg

ābi	χenṭ	ārek	ḥer - n	au - k
left.	Tread	then	upon us,	thou

reχ - θā - n	enen (ān)	semā - ā	tu	ān
knowest us.	Not	will I question	thee,	saith

ȧri	āa	en	useχt	θen	[ȧ]n ȧs
the guardian	of the door	of		hall	this, except

teṭ - nek	ren - ȧ	sa	ȧbu	tār
thou sayest	my name.	Discerner of hearts,		searcher of

χat	ren - k	semȧ - ȧ	tu	ȧref
reins,	is thy name.	I will question thee		then.

nimā	en	neter	ȧmi	unnut - f
Who	is	the god	dwelling in	his hour?

teṭ - k	set	en	māau	taui
Speak thou it.			The recorder of	the two lands.

peti trȧ	su	māau	taui
Who then is	he	the recorder of	the two lands?

Teḥuti	pu	māȧ	ȧn	Teḥuti	i - nek
Thoth	it is.	Come,	saith	Thoth,	come thou

er   må   i - nå   åå   er   semåt
hither (?).   I come   advancing   to   the examination.

peti   trå   χert - k   åu-å   åb - kuå
What then is   thy condition?   I,   I am pure

45.   em   χu   neb   åu   χu - nuå
from   evil   all.   I am   protected

em   šentet   ent   åmu   hru - sen
from the baleful acts of   those who live in   their days,

enen (ån)   tuå   emmå - sen   semå - å   åref
not   am I   among them. I have examined then

46.   tu   nimå   en   haat   em   sešet
thee.   Who   goeth down   into the flame,

ånbut-s   em   ååretu   unnu
its walls are [surmounted] with   uraei,   being

satu - f	em	ennu	ui
his paths	in	that same	lake ?

sebi	pu	Ásär	pu	uṯa	ȧrek
The traverser		Osiris	is.	Come forward	then,

māketu	smā - θȧ	ȧu	tau - k
verily	thou hast been examined ;	is	thy bread

em	uṯat	ḥeqt	em	uṯat	ȧu
from the *utchat*,	and	[thy] beer	from	the *utchat*,	are

per - tu	nek	χeru	ṭep	ta
brought out	to thee	sepulchral offerings	upon	earth

em	uṯat	......	su	er - ȧ
from	the *utchat*.	Hath decreed it	he	for me.